Stephanie Dickinson

Girl Behind the Door:

A Memoir of Delirium and Dementia

Rain Mountain Press
New York City

First Printing January 2017

ISBN: 978-1-4951-0608-8

Rain Mountain Press
www.rainmountainpress.com
New York City

Printed in the USA
Copy editor: Cindy Hochman of "100 Proof" Copyediting Services
Cover photographs: Eleanor Leonne Bennett
Cover Design: Sarah McElwain
Interior Design: Jonathan Penton

Other Books by Stephanie Dickinson

Half Girl

Corn Goddess

Road of Five Churches

Lust Series

Port Authority Orchids

Heat: An Interview with Jean Seberg

Love Highway

The Emily Fables

For my brothers
Joel and Brett

Contents

Hauntings in Sepia

I hold a photograph. It is my parents' wedding. 1946. We're in a century of tomorrow, the American Century. The World War's been won, and V-E and V-J Days celebrated. America's economy, its infrastructure undamaged by firebombing and nightly raids, its people fed and far from the scourge of fighting armies, and its returning veterans about to be educated by the G.I. Bill, is ready to explode. The calamity of Europe–two stones, one atop the other–clears the way for the rise of the United States.

The bride is older than the groom, not a teenager like her mother and aunt had been on their wedding days. Florence wears her shoulder-length auburn hair in loose curls, with bangs and waved sides. Her dark blue eyes look directly at the photographer. I know their color, but in the portrait, more varied in its tones than sepia, I'd only be sure of my father-to-be Philip Osborne Dickinson's black eyes, which shine from behind his wire-rims. His black hair, cut short and combed back from his forehead, shows its widow's peak. He wears a pinstriped blue suit and a maroon tie. Much like the suit he'll be buried in. His face reveals sensitivity and intelligence, the qualities most important to my mother. Her gown's all satin and lace, a waist-length trimmed veil, and the flourish of train and Stephanotis. A gown so lovely it makes the insects go silent, like when the sun passes behind a cloud.

Unlike the generation before, my mother has traveled far from the Iowa farm. Escaping the claustrophobia of gunny sacks and chores, she'd found fulfillment in the Red Cross during World War II, and while she was stationed in California, five men had proposed. Those years were the happiest of her life, when she was *Miss Telecky*, and worked as a salaried director of recreation. Although the groom is a Chicago boy, he's spent four years as a Merchant Marine, lifting oil drums on tankers while sailing between Brazil and North Africa, hauling precious fuel cargo across the Atlantic to feed the Allied war machine. Soon he will study conservation biology, but the lifting will come back to haunt him when doctors discover the weakness of his heart and its shrunken aorta.

Her war over too, Florence is teaching high school math in Reno, Nevada, when the two meet at a church bonfire hotdog roast. My mother roasts hers until its skin blackens, and his first words to her are, "You must like carbon." He's seven years younger than his bride. "Women live longer than men," he reportedly said. Did he mean that, based on the actuarial tables, he and Florence could be expected to live about the same number of years? My mother will live 64 years longer than him.

They've both journeyed a great distance to find their spouse, and Florence has brought him home to the same country church where her aunt and uncle, Josie and Joseph, had wed. Josie is her father's sister, and Joseph, her mother's brother. After the ceremony, the newly married couple drives in the green Hudson to Lasswell Studios (was it once Reid Studio?) in Cedar Rapids for their wedding portrait. Tin cans rattling from the bumper, JUST MARRIED soaped over the doors. Photographers do not travel; the wedding party comes to them. Here at Lasswell's, in their happiness, they face the camera. Florence's sister is matron-of-honor and Philip has chosen his brother-in-law to be his best man. The privations of war are too close at hand to tempt the fates with an abstentious display of bridesmaids and groomsmen.

I put the photographs back into the shoebox and stretch out on the bed. I try to rest, but I am haunted. Under my lids are my mother's open eyes, their milky blue irises that don't see, although she seems to be staring at me. Her head lies on a pillow that is missing its pillowcase. A flat pillow, not like the feather pillows my great-grandmother filled with the plumage of long-ago geese. At last I fall asleep, one of those shallow sleeps that seems a continuation of the day. I am in my mother's room. The air conditioner is turned to high, and cold mists the window. Under the thin blanket, my mother is again naked. I'm looking at the tag on her pillow that says *Rest-a-Head.* I try to hug the woman, who throws out her arm and grips the bed's metal side as if she is about to drown. From her mouth, the darkness makes a sound. It forces its way out of her. Not from her gut or chest, but deeper; so deep it must hurt. A sound that smells of dirt, that comes from the black furrows of the earth. I bend to her ear. "It's Stephanie, Mother. I'm here."

Hole in the Trees

I am in flight on American Airlines from New York City to Iowa. I'll remember this drowsiness, holding my limbs against my body in the brightness above the clouds, my head pressing the window as Chicago's needle-like towers on the shore of Lake Michigan come into view. I wonder if my mother is alive.

The plane descends, and we land with a bounce.

It is Saturday. I worry that I may arrive too late. I have two hours before my puddle-jumper flight into Cedar Rapids leaves at the opposite end of O'Hare. I keep walking, seeking the quiet in the outer limits of the airport, past the circus of burritos and fat-crust pizzas. I buy a green tea from Starbucks, sit at a plastic table, and unfold the color printout of a photograph my brothers have e-mailed me. Florence had lived in her own apartment at Village Ridge, an assisted living facility, until two months ago, when aides discovered her bedroom in disarray; clothes strewn over the floor and a lamp knocked over–the minutiae of a solar eclipse. After Florence was found wandering the hall, thinking it was time for breakfast in the middle of the night, the staff moved her down to the Memory Care Unit, where the glass doors are controlled by access codes. Strange stories began to circulate. Florence of the Memory Care Unit wasn't the same Florence who'd lived upstairs. For the first time, my brothers used the words *dementia* and *delirium.*

The tea tastes of a hundred degrees. A hot summer Sunday afternoon, restless knee-high July corn.

My gaze returns to the photograph. It's a close-up of Florence between her two sons. There's grass behind them, so they're on a picnic; Joel in sunglasses, the handsome elder son, dark-haired, tanned, his arm around her shoulders, and Brett, bearded, graying, a man of such essential goodness that it radiates from him. Both are smiling. I touch my mother's face and the yellow of her scarf. The sun on the grass is like pieces of scarf picked apart by anxious fingers. "Don't always show your teeth when someone takes your picture. Try instead for a pleasant expression," she'd always advised. And it is her expression that chills me. I've never seen this woman before–the one whose eyes don't open all the way, whose blue irises are milky-gray and fading. Each muscle seems about to leap through her skin; there is such strain on her face, as if she is doing everything to keep herself from crying out. Is she staring through the exterior into her interior, the world long before her children were born? Once, at Stone City Park, we sat at the picnic table, Florence leaning on her elbow, hand under her chin, staring into the quaking aspens. "What are you looking at, Mom?" She didn't break her gaze. "That hole in the trees."

⁂

I walk to the gate for the 36-seat airplane that will take us to Cedar Rapids. The young, edgy, and hip don't get on this flight. There's meekness in their carriage, these Iowa-bound passengers with wholesome, aging faces. Although it is June, I see their eyes stamped with the raw overcast of winter drizzled over fence lines, a winter that doesn't believe in summer, a winter that brings wither and creak.

Barns down broken lanes. Beheaded windmills. We're flying into the belly of the heartland. Land of Tubby's sandwiches and Tinkerbell Car Wash. The Blue Kettle Café, where the cuisine features sweet-sour aqua pickle relish, Jell-O marshmallow salad that tastes like a wound, bacon bits, and croutons. Vegetable soup, a lukewarm orange, where an occasional green bean floats. Slices of white cake decorating slabs of powdered sugar frosting.

The plane stays at low altitude. I study what is said to be the richest soil on earth. The black loam looks dried out, with a parched, yellowy cast to it. Furrows cut, sown, and reaped. Are the fields wearing out after being endlessly raped for corn production? Agri-business rules this land of my great-grandparents. The few independent farmers who are left after the great sell-offs of the 1970s survive by corn lust. The god Ethanol. Prices keep rising. Corn is political. Pesticides are killing earthworms. The lowly earthworm that plows the soil by tunneling through it, opening pathways for water to reach plant roots. The old patchwork-quilt squares of family-farm fields are gone. How the Chippewa and Sauk and Fox native peoples must have grieved seeing the pioneers' oxen and plows. The great root system of the prairie grasses destroyed. Clouds of prairie chickens cast out. Now, too, the farm fences are gone, unbroken acre upon acre upon acre all belonging to the few. Mono-agriculture. The breadbasket emptied.

⁂

The Eastern Iowa Airport lies nine miles from Cedar Rapids, and the concrete runways are poured over fields that once belonged to my Buresh relatives. This is Telecky and Buresh country. My mother was born Florence Ruth Telecky. On Sunday night, she became unresponsive and stopped breathing. The Village Ridge staff called 911 and my brother Joel followed the ambulance to Mercy Hospital. There she began to breathe normally and was eventually released. The nurses wrapped Florence in a white blanket and Joel drove her back to the Memory Care Unit. The next day, the hospital called. Her low blood pressure was a sign of pre-active dying. They suggested Hospice. On Tuesday she rallied and ate two Salisbury steaks and potatoes, and finished off her dinner with chocolate ice cream. Joel seemed encouraged that our invincible, indomitable mother would once again rise to the occasion. "We still may see her reach triple digits," my brother assured me. Florence lacks just a year and three months before reaching her century mark.

I walk into the terminal, where my best friend from high school is waiting. She lifts her arms and waves both hands. Cynthia resembles her younger self, her 14-year-old self, the age when we met. I was new to the school and, because of a beauty mark on my chin, some of my classmates called me *Morocco Mole.* Cynthia drew pictures of me with a marble-sized mole on my chin and enormous lips.

"You look beautiful, Cynthia," I say. Her fine brown hair reaches to the small of her back. Like her father, whose head had never gone white, her shining tresses are without a single gray strand.

"I'm fat. Alcohol fat," she says, patting her hips. Her tanned skin glows against her wide white smile.

"You haven't gained a pound," I tell her. She takes my bag and slings it over her shoulder, and I follow her out. I'm home.

"Here, use my cell phone," she says, once we're settled in her SUV. "Call your mother. Tell her you'll be there soon."

We drive into the countryside that, at ground level, seems a blaze of vegetation; fields rowed with corn, the fat and juice of chlorophyll. Green Eden.

I make the call. The phone rings and rings.

On the eighth ring, the phone is knocked off its receiver. A banging, crackling. It's not the well-modulated "hello" of my mother's voice, the syllables given their due, but a jumble of discordant sounds. A groan, a mutter. "Mom, it's Stephanie. I'm on my way." Whatever I'm hearing has the texture of static. Her words bump into each other, careen wildly, bursting apart. Then her voice returns for two sentences. "Thanks for calling. I'm going back to bed now." Perhaps she doesn't have her hearing aids in. At least she's alive, and from what Joel says, she'll likely rebound and be up for a picnic in a few days.

My friend takes Interstate 380 North into Cedar Rapids; to the south is the Ely blacktop that leads to the farm where I grew up.

⁂

If Florence had picked me up at the airport, as she'd done until the last few years, we would have taken the blacktop. She'd be waiting in the terminal, and as soon as she saw me, after a quick hug, would tug at the strap of my shoulder bag. "Let me carry that."

I'd protest. "No, Mom, I can carry it."

Shaking her head, she'd roll her eyes. "You carried it on your one arm all the way from New York. I want to carry it now."

We'd argue, she in her late eighties, me in my forties, over who would carry the load from the gate to the parking lot. "Oh, you're so bullheaded!" she'd say, stomping her foot.

I'd give in, her will stronger than mine. Florence, still coloring her hair brunette, was cute, but smaller, in her black stretch pants and yellow shell sweater, in her white sandals and clip-on earrings, her clip-on sunglasses. And, so, my shrinking mother would shoulder my heavy bag, and out we'd lurch into the green shine of Iowa, the middle-aged daughter trailing after. I would follow her to the rusted-out white car, so battered that my brothers said it tilted up in 19 directions. She insisted that the vehicle would last as long as she did, and no one could convince her to throw away money just for show.

Once, after settling into the worn burgundy front seat, I had said she looked pretty. "Oh, nerts," she'd remarked. "I am old meat. Now put your seat belt on. And we'll just keep still." Before she'd turned the ignition, the clip-on sunglasses descended over her glasses and she searched for the parking ticket.

"Mom, let me pay for parking," I'd offered.

"No, you're not." She'd unzipped her purse and balls of crumpled Kleenex tumbled out. "This is my car. I'm paying." From her beaded lime-green coin purse, eight quarters jingled. We drove past the metal sculpture of five children–black, red, yellow, brown, and white–holding hands and skipping. "Honestly, what they gave for that ugly thing. Now we're not going to talk, so I can concentrate." I felt the red flush of anger at being told to be quiet after having flown thousands of miles. I would forever be the child under her command. She never stopped talking.

We would travel the blacktop until the Buresh turnoff, and then continue onto gravel road. By Zacek's one-hundred-year-old farm, she would slow the car and point into the field of prairie grass. "Luther and I danced there. At the Amana Supper Club, before it burned down." Then she would park the car on the shoulder, and we'd get out and climb up the ditch that brimmed with reeds and cattails to the barbed wire fence; she, stepping on the bottom strand and pulling up the middle strand so I could pass through. A gesture so country. She would go back to the car while I walked into her past. The loveliness she'd been at 25. Her blue eyes and auburn hair, her full lips and large breasts, her shapely legs. *A European look,* Joel had said. *Imagine how Mom and Aunt Patsy stood out then beside all the bumpkins.*

"Luther was the best dancer," she would say, when I returned to the car. "My father didn't like him." Luther Worley, musical, good-looking like the Czech men of that era, blue eyes and dark blond hair, a Clark Gable mustache; the one she wanted to marry, but would not, because he couldn't stick with a job or with college.

The only thing he could stick with was her. He'd given her a seed pearl on a gold chain. "You have my heart," he'd said. But the Mediterranean Sea had swallowed his heart during the Battle of Italy, an Army pilot missing since July of 1944.

We'd ride by the Buresh Cemetery, the pines and shagbarks clustered together like the dead. The old stones of the forefathers grazing next to the creek. Iowa summers–the most beautiful in the world. Ditch lilies swimming in the long, shining grasses, and on their stems, orange trumpets.

⁂

My friend waves to me as she drives away. I have arrived at Village Ridge, the assisted living facility my mother has called home for years. I tell the aide in the outer lobby that I'm here to visit Florence. The Memory Care Unit's doors operate by a push-button code, and the aide taps in the five digits. The glass doors lock behind me. There's a different odor here; muskier, closed-in.

The residents sit in the inner lobby in Queen Anne chairs. There's a TV room, a card room, and snack machines, but the white-haired men and women seem to favor the chairs where they are never out of sight of the doors. The free-to-come-and-go world. Enviously watching visitors leave, the stragglers of The Greatest Generation wait for death. I will learn that, in the almost two months my mother has lived in this unit, she has pounded on the glass doors to be let out. "I'm an educated woman," she'd cried. "A teacher!"

The medication cart is stalled in the middle of the hall. Plastic sippy cups and tumblers hold the evening meds: the antidepressants and tranquilizers, the blood thinners and nitroglycerin patches, the eye drops for macular degeneration, potions christened with "v's" and "x's" and "z's," the brain chemistry-altering Ativan and Xanax, pharmaceutical names chosen for their high-tech/ancient Greek sounds. Like swallowing one of Jupiter's moons. Io. Europa. Or Saturn's Hyperion. I ask the nurse in dark blue scrubs and soft-soled shoes, shaking capsules into paper cups, where Florence's room is. Angie, a black RN with high cheekbones and box braids that fall loosely around her face, looks up. We recognize each other from last year when I had visited, when Mother had had her own apartment upstairs. Angie tells me it's the first room right down the hall. Room 13. Unlucky number. I feel her eyes follow me. The door is closed and I pause before opening it. I take my first steps into the room, and feel the cold as the June weather retreats.

A young, pretty aide follows me into the room. As I approach the groaning woman on the bed, I notice anklets, slacks, and a print blouse in a pile on a chair. "Your mother keeps taking her clothes off," the ponytailed aide explains.

The woman lies naked, rubbing her face with the palm of her hand.

Thumbnails

I find myself in a room of white walls, a sliding glass window, and beige carpet. A room that can never be a home. On the walls, my brothers have tried to disguise the blank expanses. There are the framed *Cedar Rapids Gazette* Sunday Supplement photos of a single mother and her three energetic youngsters and their remodeled farmhouse. The donkey, Jack, stares lazily (sullenly) at the photographer while chauffeuring two cats on his back. My brothers cradle chickens. We stand on the hill in a field overlooking our grandmother's farm a quarter mile away. She owns all this land; her farmhouse, whose roof we can see, and the one we live in. My brothers look like ragamuffins; their burr heads are barbered badly by Florence's electric clippers and they're outfitted in flannel shirts and baggy corduroy pants. But at least their clothes are new. I wear an older cousin's turquoise-pink dress and it swims over my awkward 9-year-old body, a fat girl's ballooning dress that a can-can petticoat must have rounded out when it was new. Only Florence looks attractive, in her teacher clothes–a green sweater and brown skirt–her auburn hair loose and medium-length, with her bangs swept up. The late 1960s and 1970s are out there at the edge of the cornfield: sex and drugs, rebellion, rape; all of it. Perhaps that's what my brother is pointing at. These are the days Florence teaches the rough kids at Roosevelt Junior High. She takes a peanut butter sandwich wrapped in wax paper each day for lunch, while the other teachers buy theirs in the cafeteria. She's a lone breed in 1963. A single, commuting, working mother of three. We don't yet argue, but I complain about the handed-down clothes. "You have beautiful clothes," she'd admonished. "What I wouldn't have given to wear such beautiful clothes. I had two awful dresses and wore long underwear with them when I walked to country school. It was the Depression, and my folks didn't have money."

It's easier looking at the mother on the wall than the mother on the bed.

Florence lies there, twisting and turning. I'll later learn that this is called *terminal restlessness.* Her eyes are almost closed and her mouth ajar, as if it has to stay partly open for the groaning to come out. Like a fist trying to be born. I can see that she has her two denture plates in. Only her front bottom teeth are her own. A month and a half ago, she had phoned me at five in the morning, frantic. She couldn't find her teeth, and she was sure some kid had stolen them. *Kid?* "Mom, no one would steal your teeth," I'd tried to comfort her. She had never called me on a workday that early. I worried that she was losing her sense of time.

I stroke her arm and gaze at her bottom front teeth. Slightly crooked, not badly discolored. Seven years old when those permanent teeth erupted into her mouth, the year would have been 1919. Woodrow Wilson was president.

I lightly squeeze her right hand. For all her many boyfriends attracted by her feminine qualities, she has farm-girl hands. I do too. Large, almost mannish fingers, she rarely polished her nails, although now they wear a garish puce color. Her thumbnails, especially, have slight ridges, like corduroy. I miss seeing those ridges. I want to take the polish off.

She groans, clutching the blankets around her. "Me a good Christian," she says softly. A girl's voice. And then her words disappear into the moaning.

"Yes, you are a good Christian. Yes, you are," I say, over and over. I squeeze her hand, feel its warmth, the blood flowing through. Is she fighting such apparitions that she must protect herself? A talisman. A clove of garlic against death. "Me a good Christian!" Are those the words that can halt the dementia hallucinations? The English teacher, in her peril, forgetting her grammar.

It's shivering cold in this room. This is the first time she hasn't known me, the first time I've ever seen her in bed naked in the afternoon. Her body keeps turning and twisting; her hand picks at something on her chin.

The more I look at her hands, the more I hate what the aides have done. Puce. The color is laughing at us. As if someone had pounded her nails with a hammer and bruised them. Dark grayish-purple. These hands had learned Braille so that she could teach at the Iowa Sight Saving School (the blind school). These fingers had painted the farmhouse; refinished ancestral furniture, rubbing steel wool into chair arms, scraping down to the bone; these hands had hung clothes on the line under the green sun, and these hands had endlessly corrected student papers. Summers, these hands had planted sweet corn and tomatoes, had pulled weeds. Summers, Florence dressed in halters, bought when Bette Davis and Joan Crawford queened Hollywood. Summers, I had seen what three pregnancies had done to her once-beautiful body, the thicket of blue veins on the backs of her legs. I glimpsed the scar where the surgeon's knife had slit her stomach three times.

"Mom, Mom," I keep repeating. "Maybe you should sit up and put pajamas on." I open her dresser drawer and find purple flannels printed with blue-rimmed clouds, the kind a girl might wear. I help her to sit up; then, lifting her leg, I manage to scoot her foot inside the bottoms. I end up with both her feet inside one leg of the flannel pajamas. Thankfully, Diana, the Filipino nurse, knocks lightly and walks into the room. The aides always knock to announce themselves.

"Florence," she says. "Shall we put your pajamas on?"

Is Florence awake or asleep? Even sitting up, I can't tell. I ease her pajama bottoms over her feet and then up to her knees. Diana pulls them the rest of the way to her waist. Her calves are hers still, but the flesh on her thighs seems to flow from her bones like water. She is small as a bird, a child. She is breakable. I've never loved her more. After she is clothed, I ask Diana, not Florence, if she can go to the toilet.

"Maybe she needs to go to the bathroom," I say. "I think she might be less frightened sitting up."

Diana takes my mother's left arm and I take her right, and slowly we escort her to the toilet. Wobbly, but not terribly unsteady, none of us yet knows it is the last walk she'll take in her life. Florence cups her groin as if something hurts her, as if she is afraid of not making it. We slowly lower her onto the seat. She is so light now, skin and bones. There are no doors to the bathrooms in the Memory Care Unit. Everything is wide open. Diana's gentle voice coaxes her. "Florence, do you have to go?" And then she does. She understands something.

Back in bed, the deep groaning begins again; the flailing arms grasp the metal bed-rail, as if she is once again falling into the blackness she's always feared.

"Maybe I won't go to heaven if I don't forgive Joel's wife. I'll do it, but not yet," she had said to me on the phone about a year ago. Daisy, her ex-daughter-in-law, she blamed for not treating her son like a husband.

"Can't you give her anything for her anxiety?" I ask Diana, whose dark brown eyes widen. "Please?" I rub my mother's back. I try to hold her hand, but she pulls it away.

The moaning seems to inhabit her, and now the dread is so great, she panics. She grabs at the handrail that must be keeping her safe.

"Florence," Diana murmurs into her ear. "I'm going to give you your lorazepam." The nurse bends over the bed, her long black hair bending too. It's not a pill, nothing to swallow, but an eyedropper of liquid squirted under Florence's tongue. A benzodiazepine-class drug, like Xanax or Valium. Another moan.

"Has she eaten today?" I ask.

"She had soup yesterday," Diana answers. "But your mother has stopped swallowing."

Stopped swallowing? I try to digest her words. I wonder where Joel is. He's not picking up his cell phone. Likely he's in his car driving where reception is poor, and he's been in Iowa for weeks, shouldering our mother's illness on his own. He deserves time away. I am the prodigal daughter who needs to be initiated into our mother's deterioration.

Diana gently repeats, "Yes, your mother is no longer swallowing. We're moistening her mouth." She picks up what looks like a lollipop, but it's a pink sponge. There is a plastic sack full of individually wrapped sponge lollipops. She dips it into a tumbler of water and tries to swab the roof of my mother's mouth. "Florence, I'm just moistening your mouth. Can you bite down? Bite down." And she does bite down.

We are alone, and I hug my mother and kiss the top of her head.

Her eyes are neither open nor closed when she says, in a well-modulated voice, "Don't mess up my hair." I'm stunned. In the midst of this forest of animal sounds, she has found her old voice. The imperative case. That which gives advice or instructions; that which expresses a command. The imperative case is her natural water, the language pool in which she prefers to bathe. *Don't mess up my hair.* Now? Hair has always been important to her. She is the only resident of Village Ridge with auburn hair, and she considered herself lucky to have good, thick hair her whole life long; no bald spots or thinning patches. "Your hair looks like a bushel basket," she used to say. "Let me trim the ends." But, lately, her complaint had changed. "Your hair looks so thin. Mine has always been thick. You wash it too much."

A month and a half ago, Lola, her hairdresser, who has been coming by for the three years since Florence stopped driving, took her to the salon for coloring and a wash and set. She noticed my mother's disorientation, and went to the office to tell them she was worried about my mother being alone. She'd never seen someone deteriorate so fast. I was in New York City, working at what Florence called my *dead-end job.* I was not there to help my mother. I never was.

At my mother's hairline, a half-inch of white shows.

Florence suddenly cries, "Mother! Father!"

Mother. Father. Her gene pool–the descendants of Czech settlers from Bohemia. The patriarch and his seven sons, intent on avoiding the Austro-Hungarian military service, immigrated during the American Civil War, barely missing the draft riots. They bought Iowa farms outright, hundreds of acres; they began building farmhouses and planting orchards. The indigenous people, like the native grasses and animals, had been forced off the land.

In the 1830s, white settlers could claim Iowa land, but within six months they needed to build a cabin or break five acres of land, or five acres enclosed by a good fence, not to be left unoccupied. Five acres by five acres. By the 1860s, when my forebears immigrated, land was selling at $30 dollars an acre. In 1907, when my grandfather built his barn, he was 20, and owned 160 acres of the best soil on earth.

⁂

I call Rob from Florence's room using her amplified corded phone with glow-in-the-dark numbers. Three rings blurt off in the apartment that Rob and I share in Manhattan's East Village, a five-flight walk-up tenement. I sit at her desk, which once belonged to my grandmother, on a wooden chair made by my grandfather. *I love you, chair. I love you, desk.* Who would have guessed that of all the chairs in Florence's life, this hard-backed wooden one would be her last? It is as if my grandparents are here. The rings go unanswered, and then I try Rob's cell phone. Although we're not married, Rob jokingly refers to himself as a house husband, as well as a poet and editor. He picks up on the second ringtone. Florence is clutching at the bed railing, her mouth not making words but groans. Both of her still-strong hands tighten around the railing as if she is sinking into quicksand.

He hears the moaning behind me, the animal sounds that fill the room.

"What is that?" he asks, shocked.

"That's Mom groaning. She's terrified."

He can't reconcile the groaning woman with the feisty, spirited one who still climbed hills in her 90s and who cooked for him many times during our Iowa visits.

I tell him I have to go. I just wanted to let him know I have arrived safely.

I hold her hand and try to bring her back. I tell her that Rob wishes her well on this journey she is undertaking. A kaleidoscope of images are borne up. They erupt.

Florence at 8 years old standing in her father's old chore boots by the one-room school. The teacher crows, *First-grade reader forward.* She slumps, she bulges; she tries and tries, but she is too shy to recite, and when she opens her mouth, it is the potbelly stove hissing and belching green woodsmoke that smells the air with watery onions and skunk. *Are you asleep? Look at me.* It is 5:30 a.m. She is 11. Before school she milks four cows, lifts and drags the cans to the dirt road. Maybe this is what she's trying to do in her bed, lift and drag. She bumps her head so many times on the ice before the long-tongued wagon comes, she sees stars. At 6:30 p.m. she brings in the kindling. Buckets and buckets of corncobs she shoves down the splintered lips of the woodbox. For heat she takes a cob and soaks it in kerosene. Still, she freezes dribbling water from the tea kettle over her budding breasts. There's 15-year-old Florence at the July 4th picnic down by the creek. She sits alone, far from the hunyak boys.

Red Ball Road

Joel enters our mother's room in the Memory Care Unit, wearing beige Bermuda shorts and a matching shirt printed with tiny camels and palm trees. His legs are tanned and he wears sunglasses, as if he'd been riding the bike trails of Khon Kaen in Northern Thailand. He's handsome and looks younger than his 59 years, an unimaginable number to the Joel, Brett, and Stephanie seated at a card table in a late 1950s snapshot, drinking lemonade and scowling into the sun. He carries a jar of green tea in a decorative silver can. "Joel is smart," Florence always said. "He has such a good brain." And he does. He graduated high school at 16, and went straight to college and majored in physics.

From Florence's 1957 diary: "We stopped at Uncle Fred's on our way home. Joel put a wood puzzle together so fast that Fred stood in wonder." Once, she mentioned that Joel was the smartest of her children. Brett was her favorite, the middle child like she had been–girl behind the door, the forgotten one. And I had been a good baby and a rebellious, disobedient teen.

He lowers the metal grille and sits on our mother's bed. When her moaning starts, he pats her back. It's the moaning of a bleak, overcast day. The song of the oldest water at the barn cistern's bottom. "How long has this been going on?" he asks me, his sunglasses still on. Perhaps he is more comfortable behind their dark lenses.

"Since I got here," I answer. Diana listens as she fills Florence's water glass.

He raises the metal grille and moves to the Queen Anne chair, shifting the doll with the orangey teased hair over. The chair and the doll must have come with the room. While the doll is peering at me with her indigo eyes, I mull over what Diana had said earlier. "Your mother is no longer swallowing." Under a footstool, three pairs of Florence's shoes wait for their next wearing: brown loafers, rubber-soled canvas slip-ons, and a pair of Hush Puppies. She's left the shape of her feet in the loafers, along with her nylon knee-highs. Her glasses are folded in the pencil tray on her desk.

"We can't keep letting her moan like this, can we? Is that what's on the menu for tonight?" he addresses Diana, who's about to leave.

I stand next to the bed, stroking our mother's shoulder as she blinks, showing pieces of her milky eyes.

"Joel," Diana says in her soft voice, "if you want your mother's medication adjusted, you'll have to call Hospice."

"I'll do that, then," he says, picking up his cell phone. Joel has never bowed easily to authority. I remember the boy who called our uncle, the dignified professor who wore pressed white shirts even on his Iowa vacations, "John," not "Uncle John," and the stir it had caused. I have no memory of the boy, who had been 6 when our father died, being delivered the news. "When I told Joel that Daddy was dead in Chicago, he wouldn't stop screaming. I should have hugged him," Florence had said much later. "But I didn't. I felt so bad about Daddy, I went into the bedroom to pack." Now I think of the small boy wanting more than anything for his mother to take back those wretched words. What was the difference between "John" and "Uncle John" in a world where a sentence could announce a father's death?

Diana nods to us and eases the door shut behind her. We are with our mother, the woman who loved her children too much, who never felt comfortable unless she was in charge. "Most of the time you three children come to see me, you spend all your time entertaining yourselves," she'd written me. Does she know we are here? I have never wanted to be in charge of anyone, not even myself. And when I did drive the car of selfhood, I crashed the vehicle.

I am alone with my eldest brother.

Three years separate us; nothing now, but then, a chasm. I was in awe of him. Once, I came to his rescue. He was teasing Jack, the donkey, and in a lightning flash, Jack opened his muzzle wide and took my brother's whole hand into his mouth. While Jack's enormous teeth seemed about to bite down and sever my brother's hand from his wrist, his angry eyes were still undecided. Frantically, I tried to unclamp his clenched jaw, and it was a standoff until I offered him a handful of shelled corn.

Joel is thumbing through his cell phone's recently called numbers. "I've taken strolls around here on purpose to see how much attention Mom gets," he says, lacing his sentences with words that hint at his dry wit. "Once I had to walk outside in the parking lot before I found anyone. They had automatic access to her bank account, but we've cut that off." He takes off his sunglasses, letting them dangle from his neck on a glasses guard. Brown eyes, much like my own, stare at me. "You can be nice to the aides, but I need to be tough. Don't you know Mom's the second-longest resident of The Villages? She's paid over half a million in rent here. They should be treating her like a queen, not shutting the door and letting her moan."

And it's true, isn't it? When I arrived, I found Florence naked and moaning behind a closed door. Joel tells me that when my middle brother, Brett, had visited in early June, the woman whom they encountered wasn't their mother. Her talk swam together in a flow of the incoherent. The new mother, unlike the modest mother of old, began undressing in front of them; my religious mother, who read from the Bible at the breakfast table and aloud before bed, who sent me Anchor pamphlets each month for years, had lost her taste for God. When my gentle brother Brett started reading from the Bible to her, her face darkened. "Go read to your mother," she grimaced. Brett turned to her with his warm brown eyes and took her hand. "But you are my mother." She snatched her hand back. "Go read to your mother."

Sometimes the old mother or sometimes the recognizable one of the long decline would appear. I spoke to her once on the phone. On her last picnic with Joel, she had walked, having to stop three times, but walking all the same, into the park behind her retirement complex. Thomas Park, acres and acres of quaking aspen and willow, the sound of the trees like the rustling of a river, hills where deer and wild turkey slipped from the brush to show themselves, and then disappear. After they ate, Joel put his arms around her and they hugged. She held tightly on to him. When they broke apart, she said, "You must meet my sons. You'd like them."

"I'm going into the hall to try to contact Hospice," Joel tells me. "They're a business now. They charge Mom's Medicare $150 a day whether they visit or not."

⁂

Joel had majored in physics at Dana College in Blair, Nebraska, a college founded by the Danish on the windswept plains. Joel had dated and fallen in love with a blonde co-ed. All the while, she'd secretly been engaged to a Marine deployed in Vietnam. When the Marine returned to the States, he'd asked her to set the wedding date, and she did. Joel drove frantically between Iowa and Kansas City, speaking to the girl's mother at length, presenting his case. The co-ed married her Marine, and Joel never dated a

Caucasian girl again. Florence wondered whether this early hurt had made him gun-shy of relationships that led to the altar. Instead, he'd settled in California, bought Pacific Cash Register Company, drove a Jaguar, and lived in a Japanese modernist home in San Rafael. He'd met an inventor and wrote a physics book called *The Death of Rocketry*. He had dated a Miss Hawaii, followed by a string of quality women. Cuban, Puerto Rican, Chinese, Filipino. In the mid-'90s he'd fallen in love with the astonishingly beautiful daughter of a political Filipino family. From a distance, my elder brother, the boy who played beneath the apple trees in our grandparents' vanished orchard, had succeeded mightily. Then came the California real estate collapse. The Pacific Cash Register Company no longer thrived. Joel roamed the world, especially Australia and Southeast Asia. Thailand. Cambodia. Vietnam. The Philippines. At last, he married. His bride, a Filipino girl decades his junior, hailed from a fishing village six hours north of Manila. While there was little money, life offered constant celebrations of marriages and births within the extended family. In the first picture I saw of her, I thought she was a child. The goblet she sat behind seemed to shade her like a tree. They'd married in the Philippines, and then married again in California. He hoped to start a family. They settled in Sacramento, where she found not one but two jobs. On Christmas Day, they'd been invited for dinner at a friend of Joel's. She insisted that my brother pay her time-and-a-half (her employer's overtime hourly rate) for the shift she'd volunteered for and would miss. I understand how like a dream the overtime pay was for someone raised without running water or shoes. And, yet, I too was taken aback.

I do not want to talk about the beauty of my relationship with Rob or mention how much Florence liked him. Rob and I have been together for thirteen years and call ourselves the B-Team. Blessedly, we live in a tenant-run building, a slum–though it *is* in Manhattan–the lobby windows stained with pigeon droppings, the tiles cracked or painted over, and marble stairs that a century of foot traffic has warped. We enjoy walking up the eight flights of stairs to the apartment we share with our two cats, Sally Joy and Vallejo. You can see where the dumbwaiter had been, where blocks of ice made the upstairs trek by pulley. Here we reside with others fortunate enough to be tenants in a rent-controlled building: the elderly brothers Asher and Herman, whose shouting matches, "You whore!" "Call the cops! Call the cops!" "Go to hell!" spill into the stairwells; and Christina, the Tenant Association president, a gruff, big-hearted woman, a Spanish-speaking Pole from Argentina whose "Screw the Bastards!" is her one-size-fits-all phrase; and Bodhan, the Russian home health aide who inherited his apartment from the elderly Pole he worked for, and some days he remodels and other days he drinks, but "sssshhh, don't tell my daughter." Except at tenant meeting free-for-alls where everyone shouts, the tenants rarely speak, or if we accidentally meet in our journeying up and down the steps, do so in hushed tones. Even the exterminator whispers, as if killing roaches is so onerous, so murderous, he prefers that residents do not answer their doors.

On our floor, we sometimes meet our next-door neighbor Stan Tin Pau on the landing, talking to our other neighbor, Frank, who carries a fishing pole that smells of the East River. Stan is the head of his household, which includes his girlfriend, their new baby, Joshua, and his girlfriend's two sisters and father. The father and sisters had been burned out of their own apartment; in the fire, the mother died and one of the sisters lost her right hand. Grizzled and gray-bearded Frank Rodriguez is a proud fisherman who consumes his catch. "Do you eat herring?" he asks me as I unlock the door and carefully turn the loose knob. "I have some if you eat herring."

Inside, our apartment runs longer than wide. The plumbing harkens back to the days of cold-water flats, and the bathroom hosts only a tub and toilet, no sink. In the kitchen, the doors to cupboards have fallen off, the ceilings are fissured, and the floors splintered. Yet, we love the homely rooms. Each window fills with sunlight and our bedroom overlooks tiny Marble Hill Cemetery, one of Manhattan's earliest burial grounds, all limestone tombstones and tulip trees. Here I live with Rob. Six-foot-one, broad-shouldered with brown hair to his chest, his blue-eyes are Mongolian skies, his handsome face is almost pretty. *Fabio* he has been called on the street, Fabio, the romance novel pin-up boy. He believes he is ugly and spent years as a teen holding his hand in front of his face. He suffers from Asperger's syndrome, with its physical and emotional discomfort; where one's own skin chafes, and holding a conversation with peers is excruciating, even simple social interaction awkward.

His interests aren't horizontal and wide-ranging, but narrow, vertical depth charges. Rob's passions are music and poetry. Growing up, he'd been bullied and shunned, and he still thinks anyone who laughs on the street is laughing at him. Thin and a runner in high school, all long legs and arms, he despises his old self, and lifts weights to assure himself that the cowering person he used to be no longer exists. I find him endlessly pleasant to look at. In his sleep there's no quietude. He moves constantly, shifting, climbing, tossing; a current that tugs the bedding out from under me; Rob, the river sleeper. Even the Paxil and Zyprexa, the psychotropic meds he's been taking in low doses for thirteen years, don't help to relax him. Many nights, as he's falling to sleep, he lunges up on his elbows, gulping in jerky breaths.

"Something's happening! Something's happening!" he cries out.

"You're okay. Everything's okay," I reassure him.

He's been unable to hold a job; his social anxiety, his temper, and his phobias interfere with his work performance. Too self-conscious to lose himself in the mechanical, he's always alert to insult–if an insult is not readily available, he'll gnaw at some trifle until it becomes one.

**

The lorazepam doesn't seem to be working. Florence flails her arms and grabs onto the metal sides of the bed. She shrieks and groans. I stand beside the bed, touching her, trying to comfort her with my presence. Joel's still in the hall on his cell, trying to reach Hospice. "Mom, you're growing young," I tell her. "How pretty you look. Even your wrinkles have disappeared." I bend over her, patting her back. "Mom, Mom," I say again and again. "Mom." I wonder if her eyes are still seeing, or if the brain is shutting off her vision.

A few days ago, my brother mentioned on the phone that Florence thought she was staying with her grandparents and going to Washington High School. That she lived on 16th Avenue in Czech Town and wanted to be taken there. She believed she was 15 years old. That would be the year she learned to play the 12-string Spanish guitar. Clusters of amber grapes had been painted on the guitar's box. She'd be walking along the Cedar River, carrying her precious instrument. The one I will steal from her when I'm 17 and give away to hooligans. She might be thinking about throwing herself into the river. Something she once let accidentally slip. Depression, the lifelong blackness she fought.

One foot in the hereafter, she'll take it all with her; her childhood, my childhood, the cob stove, and the mirrors for the threshers, the white-seamed nylons and stocking garters. She'll take the "I be cold" story. She'll take the shortcut on Red Ball Road and the adorable white dog with black tail galloping through the lawn. How hard is this thing she must do? This *being born into death.*

⁂

Florence chose to live at the newly constructed retirement complex abutting Thomas Park, where Cedar Rapids and its sister city, Marion, flow into each other. She'd passed it on her commute to Linn-Mar, where she taught junior high school English before retiring. One of the first senior living facilities in Southeastern Iowa; two-bedrooms, one-bedrooms, and studios for those 55 and up. Florence was 74 then.

Joel will take part of the night shift. He's gotten in touch with Hospice, who will visit Florence in the morning. "After Dad died, she moved us out there on the farm. I was 8 years old, the oldest. We were totally dependent on her, and you know as well as I do that she never felt comfortable unless she was in charge. I had a choice from among so many beautiful, bright women, but I was afraid I might marry someone who, deep down, was like Mom. Who would try to dominate me. Mom was hypercritical, and we absorbed all that."

I stand outside in the back courtyard, feeling the trees, the willows, and the quaking aspens' leaves swimming against each other; an opera of breeze, a twig-fest, ebony birds and tawny ones. I walk across the parking lot to Village Place, where Florence had lived for seventeen years. Joel is renting one of their visitors' studio units, and I use his key to get inside. I take the stairs to the third floor and walk down the long hall, past the familiar prints of Degas ballerinas caught in their arabesques and tutus. I stop by the door to my mother's old apartment and touch the shaded patch in the wood where the *Peace to All Who Enter* plaque had hung. A peculiar peace lay behind that door when Florence lived there. Now, a yellow tape stretches across the doorknob, as if it is a crime scene, not a remodeling site.

Sister Morphine

The next afternoon, the Hospice on-call nurse, Shauna, arrives. Everyone in summer Iowa is deeply tanned, and she looks as if she's just come from Lake Macbride–one of Eastern Iowa's rare rural parks with a lake for swimming–except she carries a beach bag stocked with thermometers and blood pressure cups and pink sponge mouth moisturizers–lollipops for the dying. This angel of merciful death wears fitted jeans and a sleeveless T-shirt.

When Shauna lifts my mother's arm to wrap the Velcro blood pressure bandage around it, Florence rises up with a cry; her upper body almost levitates as she struggles to free herself. Shauna speaks gently, trying to calm her.

"We're going to get your mother comfortable," she says. "We'll set up a medication schedule." Her hair is worn up in a bun of the whitest, most glistening cornsilk, but it is her eyebrows that draw my attention. Greta Garbo brows. Five silver studs decorate each ear and silver bracelets make her movements musical. "The nurses here will be instructed to give her lorazepam and morphine every four hours."

"What kind of pain is she in?" I ask this nurse, whose musical bracelets almost mock the solemnity of death. In her face there's no trace of the hospital beds and catheters, all the endings of a human personality. Yet, help is here.

Up and down the silver bracelets roll between her tanned elbows and wrists, and it's a lively, comforting sound.

Shauna turns and her blue eyes meet mine. "The moaning tells us she is in pain. It might be her heart. It might be that her back is uncomfortable from lying there."

"But this is her first full day in bed."

"She can't tell us in words, but her body is talking."

Does Florence know she's fighting for her life, or fighting to end her life? "I'm dying," she had said earlier, between groans. I had lied to her, although I doubt she heard as her hearing aids weren't in. "No, you're not dying," I'd said. "No, you're not!"

"I'm dying" is what my aunt kept saying during her first and last real illness, in her 94th year. My mother's older sister, Patsy, chose Hospice rather than surgery when lung cancer was diagnosed. She'd never smoked, but my uncle, the dentist, had. Her drugs of choice were anise hard candies and Fanny Farmer chocolates. "I'm dying," my aunt kept repeating, as if incredulous, or marveling at the brightness of the world dimming. After so much life, is death still unimaginable?

"Morphine every four hours," I repeat, surprised by the choice. She'd never taken a painkiller stronger than an aspirin. Anti-anxiety, yes, a tranquilizer, yes, but the elephant gun morphine? Sister Morphine is for a younger Keith Richards and his paramour, Anita Pallenberg. For a Keith Moon strolling the moonlight mile; not a member of The Greatest Generation. We nod as Shauna tells us again that every four hours Florence will receive the poppy's bliss. Until a few months ago, my 98-year-old mother, with her brown hair and scrappiness, still had a recognizable self. The slow, steady decline ended and she had toppled off the cliff into dementia. The woman who taught me phonics had lost three-fourths of her vocabulary. I will read of Hospice patients who die of morphine intoxication. I'll learn that morphine slows the breathing, then stops the breathing. But now we want calm and sleep for the woman on the bed. Liquid morphine is the elixir for the dying. The beverage served by the boatman on the River Styx.

My brother gets to his sandaled feet, clearing his throat as if to announce himself. "Tomorrow, which is Sunday, if my mother is still moaning, do we phone you? I assume you're still our contact."

Shauna nods. "I'm the on-call nurse for this weekend. After Sunday, the number I gave you is no longer active."

Joel likes to ask questions; he's interested in systems, how they operate, and in how people respond. "About how many patients are you seeing today?" he inquires. He questions her at length about where she lives (Coralville) and the geographical area she traverses to see Hospice patients. We learn that Shauna travels the entire quadrangle of Southeastern Iowa–Cedar Rapids, Marion, Hiawatha, Coralville. I can't keep from staring at her eyebrows, like tiny arcs, traces of quick bird-flight. They almost imperceptibly rise and fall as she talks. My mother, for all her striking European looks of her younger years, never plucked her eyebrows. They grew untamed over her blue eyes, which I rarely looked into until the last year of her life. Florence, ultra-conscious of her skin tone and complexion, seemed not to notice her thick eyebrows. She colored her hair, but her brows were allowed to meander. As a child, I rarely thought of my mother as pretty. She was 41 when I was born, and was older than other parents. Now, with older eyes in my head, I see that she was slender and very attractive.

Florence curls and uncurls under the sheet, drawing her knees up and extending them again. "How do you know she is dying?" my brother asks Shauna. "A week ago, we were having a picnic. Three days ago, she ate double portions at dinner." He retells the story of the two Salisbury steaks, polished off with pie and ice cream.

He settles again in the Queen Anne chair with the orange-haired, blue-eyed doll. The doll is so out of place here. Who does it belong to? A child visitor or one of the residents in their second childhood? He takes a swallow of green tea. "She's strong, and her most recent pattern is to have bad days followed by fairly normal days. I told my sister not to rule out her getting up and picnicking with us this weekend."

Shauna is collecting her blood pressure wrap and carry-pack, preparing to leave. "Your mother is dying, although not actively dying."

"There's a difference? What do you mean by *actively dying*?" Joel slips his sunglasses off, wanting to see the answer, not just hear it. His brown eyes appear darker, as if their pupils are eclipsing his irises. The whites of his eyes are tinged with red. My brother and I are both haunted by the mistakes we have made in our lives.

"If she were actively dying," Shauna says, "we would see particular processes. The mind, body, and spirit all have to work together to die because it's hard work. Florence's mind and spirit made that decision when she stopped eating. And now her body has to make that decision."

"But," Joel interrupts. "Three days ago, she ate like a horse. I sat beside her."

"Often, the dying experience a resurgence in the days before the dying begins. Their appetites return and they eat big meals. It takes a lot of energy to die, and that was likely your mother readying herself for the journey." Shauna walks toward the door, her cell phone ringing. She hands me the Hospice booklet on dying. She'll talk to the nurses on her way out.

I will hear an aide tell me that two bites of a chocolate pie had been the last solid food she had eaten. "Who doesn't like chocolate pie?" the aide winked. I will hear how she had spit her food out. How my mother had fought going to the cafeteria, stamping her foot in a characteristic gesture. "I put my foot down!" she'd huffed, shaking her head angrily.

"Florence's body has to make that decision to join the mind and spirit," Shauna says from the doorway.

So, you do not just die. Your respiration and digestion and circulation are separate solar systems that must decide to work as one. They must all drive toward extinction together. The brain fights the most to live.

"But last week we went on a picnic," my brother says, as if unable to fathom the Florence who had walked with him into Thomas Park and the woman roiling on the bed.

"Did she enjoy the picnic?" I ask.

"No," he says flatly, and follows Shauna out into the hall.

* *

Mom was "a little shy," Joel once remarked. Reserved. She smiled but did not show teeth. She socialized little with other seniors, did not play bingo because she couldn't hear the numbers, and was bored with birthday parties and sing-alongs, although she played the organ, and her soprano voice had attracted my father. Eight men had proposed to her before she chose my father, who was seven years younger than she. "She was too picky," my uncle Douglas told me. In her Red Cross years during WWII, Miss Florence Telecky graced the great military bases in California and Arizona. Countless photos show my red-lipped and smiling mother in crisp uniform, with soldiers' arms around her, her hair in the loose style of Rita Hayworth. There is something about her that the other pretty nurses and recreation workers in the '40s photos don't have–sex appeal. It's not heavy makeup or provocative body language; it's subtle, but there all the same. Full-figured. A sense of flesh. Something men responded to. That my mother was always a devout Christian made that quality all the more seductive.

Angie, the black nurse, comes in to administer the first dose of morphine. She uses an eyedropper, then lets the morphine soak into the flesh of my mother's mouth. How intimately these strangers come to know us, and in their knowing, are no longer strangers. She steps out and returns in about ten minutes to see if the groaning has ceased and to take Florence's temperature. Mother is still fighting anyone who startles her or abruptly touches her. Like she fought against the blood pressure's harmless Velcro wrap. I like Angie, and find her almond-shaped eyes and her full features handsome. I'd met her last year, and remember that she has three children; one in the military, one in college, and one in high school. I remember how kind she had been to my mother. She must be in her mid-forties, although she could pass for early thirties. "Do you think we should take her dentures out?" I ask, using the *we*, but really asking her to remove them. All my life, I've stood on the sidelines, waiting for the responsible person to act.

She snaps on rubber gloves. "Yes, they might be hurting her mouth." Bending over the bed, she speaks directly into my mother's ear. "Okay, Florence, let's take your teeth out." My mother moans when Angie reaches in to wiggle them loose, but they seem to fight to stay in her mouth. When my mother was 11 and tasked with cranking the iron handle of the butter churn–a hard job–her hand slipped and the handle recoiled, knocking out her two front teeth. I can see her in her work dress of brown or gray under an apron, her everyday boots, blood smeared over her face. Under the gray sky of kerosene light, in the midst of the Depression, her parents took her to the Ely dentist, trading freshly butchered chickens for two badly fitting front teeth. When she got her first teaching job, at $40 a month, she managed to save for pretty ones. Now her mouth will lose its teeth memories. Angie drops my mother's dentures into a plastic case near the sink and adds two tablets of Efferdent.

Later, I will berate myself for all the last sentences I missed. Maybe Florence needed to cry out in dread. Maybe her daughter and son could not stand to hear the groaning. Maybe it was for ourselves that we chose morphine.

⁂

A few weeks before her 98th birthday, my mother had crossed 1st Avenue, heading to the Short Stop convenience store. She'd walked across four of the busiest lanes of traffic in Cedar Rapids/Marion. Making it across the highway, she purchased Tylenol PM, and then forded her way back through the river of traffic but stumbled in the Village Ridge parking lot. A young man from the Short Stop saw her fall and called an ambulance. Immediately, she was taken to Mercy Hospital.

"They made a big fuss," she said to me on the phone. "I told them I was fine. I got up, didn't I? But, no, they put me in an ambulance."

I got up, didn't I? My mother had always gotten up.

When my brother Brett phoned to tell me, my first thought was that the mother who raised me would not buy Tylenol PM at the Short Stop. I took Tylenol PM for sleeplessness and had offered it to her when I'd visited. She'd always refused.

That was Florence's outward manifestation of her descent into dementia. *At least I'll always have my mind,* she'd said. And her three children believed her.

The weather had been record-breakingly hot that September day. At one time it might have been called Indian Summer. In her last decade, my mother noticed–in the periphery of her consciousness–the funny weather. Her expression for the scorching heat, the wet snow that in winter never stuck on the ground, the spring tornadoes. Never did she call it *climate change.* "We're having funny weather," she would say on the phone. "The weather's been so funny, but, then, I don't go anywhere, so what does it matter?"

The morphine has done its work, and Florence appears to be resting.

⁂

On the second night of my mother's dying, I sleep in the Memory Care Unit, in the room next to Florence's. Diane, the director of Village Ridge, has offered me its use during the deathwatch. It is the same white-walled room as my mother's, furnished with a single bed, a shower curtain, and a doorless bathroom. Joel will continue staying in the studio apartment he's renting at Village Place, across the parking lot. Together, Village Ridge and Village Place are called The Villages.

"They gave me a pretty good price on the studio," Joel says, after we kiss our mother's forehead. She smells sweet, as though the aides have just applied Moonlight Mile lotion to her face. Florence has been sleeping deeply since the every-four-hours morphine began. "After what I went through to get the damage deposit back from her old apartment, I was surprised. The Villages is a franchise. Their headquarters is in Denver. These are not the honest, kind-hearted Iowa types. I badgered them for months, and it wasn't until Mom broke her elbow in their parking lot that we got the deposit."

"Were they afraid we'd sue?" I ask.

"Sure, sure," Joel answers. "They're supposed to have some kind of lasso to rein in residents like Mom when they're running around the highway. But that's only in their brochure." He puts his sunglasses back on and I follow him through the darkened halls of the Memory Care Unit, where women with their hair on fire run through the dreams of the Alzheimer's patients. There are groans, and then a voice calls out in a Southern accent from down the hall. "Help me! Please, help me! Help me, please!"

"Should we try to find a nurse?" I ask my brother. "It sounds like that woman is frightened."

"That woman has been frightened every night since I've been here. She's another one the aides close the door on."

We pass the visitors' kitchen, where the refrigerator and stove and countertops are muted in shadow, yet their presence is soothing. The wood cabinets are homely; they are an objective reality. I want to press against the dishwasher and listen to it hum and be comforted. Everything is shifting, shape-changing, and here there is solidity. The floor tile. The sink. The rock of the refrigerator.

Again, the woman's voice cries, "Help me! Please, help me! Help me, please!"

"Joel, wait. Do you hear? We have to find one of the nurses."

He half turns. "No, we don't. She calls for help every night at the same time, and then she stops. The first time I heard it, I managed to find someone, and that's what I was told."

The door opens. A square-haired woman is standing there with wide, moon-flooded eyes, her pajama bottoms rolled above her knees, and then she wades flat-footed down the hall, as if it is flooded with water.

My brother and I walk out into the Iowa summer night, where crickets chirrup and the breeze from the quaking aspens lifts my hair. Fireflies are swimming through the parking lot like tiny flashlights nosing the dark. On off, on off. Red-gold sparks. I haven't seen this many fireflies since I was a farm child.

We stand and watch the fireflies. I wonder what our hurry was to leave this place. Iowa. Meaning *beautiful land.* Joel tells me how much our mother had helped him during his rocky marriage to Daisy. He had phoned her and talked for hours. She listened. He could not admit to his men friends that his child-bride marriage was a disaster. He'd waited until he was 50 to marry. We all had wanted to love Daisy. But we were middle-aged aliens in her 20-year-old world. "There was no one I could talk to except Mom," he repeats. "She listened for hours."

⁂

When Rob and I first hooked up with each other, after we'd met in Jill Hoffman's glass-table workshop, I was 43, and he, 27. We liked each other's writing first. I was impressed by his poetry, his amazing images and metaphor-making. His face was no K-mart parking lot overcast with cliché wire shopping carts; being in his presence was a mirror image of underwater trees–my own self peering back. We were that odd pairing, although a generation separated us, they call *kindred souls*, a rarity. Like Cathy and Heathcliff, Rob is my own spirit in another body, another sex. I'd lived with other boyfriends, and though I cared for them, we were not soulmates, we were accidents.

I'd feared how his mother and father would react to a typist who was sixteen years older than their son. And, yet, the first time I met his parents they made me feel welcome in their living room of braided rugs and sheer blue curtains, three cats asleep on the back of the couch, two more in the recliner. I felt even more welcome in their kitchen, where his mother served stuffed mushrooms, garlic bread, and lasagna, the noodles baked into a stream of melted mozzarella and ricotta. Later, his parents told Rob they liked me; I seemed very intelligent, they said.

Dementia Mother

It is Saturday still, and I think of Saturdays on the farm where I grew up. I take a journey in this small room in the Memory Care Unit. A euphemism, to put it mildly. My eyes wander the china cabinet; its porcelain tea cups, the gravy servers, the delicate ice-scrapers and gold-painted handles of another age's eating utensils. Like me, those tea cups used to live in the farmhouse on the hill. The house built by my great-grandfather Telecky in 1900.

On Saturdays, my mother has her twice-monthly hair appointment. I'm alone, and the good feeling I get from aloneness seeps through me. My brothers are with friends in town, and I watch a funnel of dust chase Florence's blue Rambler down the hill. She's off to Hilda Minor's Beauty Salon for hair coloring, plus a wash and set. Less than a mile away, the salon is built onto Hilda and Virgil's crooked house, and all around are downed trees and ruts. Sows often wallow in the middle of the narrow lane. I am 11, and Florence has just joined Parents Without Partners at the YWCA. One of the single fathers has asked her out to a dance at Armar Ballroom. My job is to clean the three-story farmhouse, upstairs and downstairs. I've dragged out the vacuum sweeper with the electric tape swaddled around its cord. I've got my bucket of vinegar water and rags, and am ready to kneel and wash the woodwork, that ledge near the floor that attracts dirt. I know which stretches are the toughest–the chore room off the kitchen that leads to the cellar and faces the coops and barn. Chicken feed and oyster shells are kept here, along with the 30-lb. bags of cornmeal we boil to make the mush to feed stray cats. There's mush, dried like a gritty sunrise, on the wall and woodwork; the mud scuff marks of chore boots; and, in my nose, the reek of wet feathers. I want to get this miserable task out of the way, and then throw the dirty vinegar water out the back door, next to the summer kitchen.

I save the living room for last. Too beautiful to ever be used, here the wallpaper is a cream ecru lace on half the walls, and then, for accent, one wall is printed with tiny gondoliers and weeping willows. On the new beige carpet are throw rugs, put down wherever anyone might consider walking. I dust the carved arms of antique furniture–matching burgundy velvet rockers and a yellow velvet loveseat. I wrap the warm, wet rag around my hand and clean the bookcase, and then I climb the buffet to wash the mirror. I stop to look at myself. Is there any prettiness in this face? Round cheeks, dark eyes encased in butterfly glasses. Without beauty, what is possible? Does it show in my features–the gravel road, the cellar where a skunk crawled into the foundation and died next to the freezer, the civet taste of lemonade and ice cream, the *me too!* brand? The buffet has hieroglyphics carved into its legs, mahogany knees like a hope chest, and mysterious forests, and in its drawers is Florence's wedding silver. Never to eat with; only for her to know they exist, forever to lie in their maroon-flannel dark, whispering silver and night. I open the silverware chest, pick out a serving spoon, and peer into its oval, and my wide cheeks fatten. Then I lift the spoon, and my cheeks thin and my brown eyes melt down the handle. No hope for this face. I yearn for pinkness, for fake go-go boots and mohair sweaters, for Loretta Young and Jackie Kennedy mothers who wear pearls and high heels, who tan and smoke cigarettes. All I yearn for is excitement somewhere far away from here.

⁂

It will be many years before I realize what I had in childhood, how I took the farm for granted, wanted desperately to move to a town, any town. I did not appreciate the sweat of my great-grandparents and grandparents, who dug the wells so we could drink our own pure water, who built the farmhouses and barns and planted the orchards, who furrowed the richest black soil on earth and coaxed from it abundance.

In late September, when I visited my mother after she'd fallen and broken her elbow, her left arm was in a cast and the aides had to help her dress. We took the Village Ridge bus to Florence's physical therapy appointment, where another, more lightweight, cast was put on. "It's still so hard," Florence complained after getting home, jimmying the stiff plastic that had been sculpted around her thumb and over her hand and forearm. "Stephanie, I don't think I can stand it. I'm so old. Why did they put this animal on my arm?" I watched her bend and break off the pieces that bothered her. I found that act defiant and courageous.

I worked in Manhattan at an accounting firm with three weeks' yearly vacation. I would take two of those weeks to visit Florence. I suspected she no longer read the *Cedar Rapids Gazette* delivered to her door each morning. Were her eyes weaker or was the print itself losing meaning for her? We sat at the table over breakfast. She hardly glanced at the obituaries, her favorite newspaper section. Her Village Ridge studio came with a refrigerator and a microwave, but no stove, no space heater in the bathroom, nothing she could start fires with.

"You gave me more oatmeal than you gave yourself," Florence accused. A strain of masochism runs in the matriarchal side of my family. Denial of the flesh its own pleasure.

"Please, Mom, I have plenty," I said.

She began spooning oatmeal from her bowl into mine.

"Stop, Mom, please."

Florence let out an exasperated sigh. "No. You gave me twice what you gave yourself." We ate toast with cherry jam that my uncle Fred had made. We argued about who had more. "I don't want so much toast," she insisted. "Eat mine. Your face is too thin." My stomach knotted. We spoke of Uncle Fred. Three months earlier, after working in his garden, Uncle Fred had gone into his house and asked his wife for an aspirin, and then, stretching out on the couch, died. My mother had loved her younger brother more than she loved herself. "Dirt is the cleanest thing there is," Florence claimed. And, so, the son of the farm had worked in dirt at the end.

"He was the best brother," she said. "He never said an unkind word to me. He would play dolls with me in the corncrib. We had two cracked plates and a cup. Then we invented games. One I remember was called *funeral*."

They would wrap their doll in a rag and pull her on a board, taking turns in the orchard giving the eulogy. I see them under the filigreed sky, among the green walnuts and apples. During the great black-and-white world, the grayness that was the Depression, the two younger children of John and Emily Telecky, playing funeral, stop to eat a wormy apple, so juicy and delicious, even the wormhole. Like biting into a blossom. "We also played baptism in the sheep trough. The ewes were blessed and their lives given to Christ." My uncle went on to become a minister.

I sat at my mother's table eating a dead man's jam so succulent, and I marveled at how the hands that had picked the cherries had vanished, yet there was this sweet red taste in my mouth. Despite everything, I was enjoying a leisurely breakfast in Iowa's green summer light. I thought of a long-ago Sunday in my uncle's church. In my family, to be a minister is to scale rock-star heights. Preaching, the pipes of the organ rising behind him, Uncle Fred stood before the congregation in his robes, his voice warm, conversational. He was six-foot-three, blue-eyed and black-haired. More than one girl had lost her heart to him. I sat in the pew between my mother and grandmother, proud that the pastor was my uncle. He told us a story of his pilot days. It was WWII when he wore the leather flyers jacket and said to his father, "I'm not going to let other men do *my* fighting." The war that altered so much in America found him in a C-47, shot down over the Hump in Burma. The Japanese had closed the Burma Road, and he was part of the U.S. Army Air Corp. mission flying supplies to China over the Himalayas, the Iowa boy in the air over 14,000-foot ridges and crags and peaks. Parachuting out of his dying plane, he landed in a tree in rugged terrain. Chinese peasants discovered him and led him to safety. Over those days, he learned the taste of strange foods. He asked for God's help and promised that if he returned from wherever he was, he would become a minister. I froze, imagining the bail-out into that icy darkness. To be tangled in a parachute and caught in a tree, to eat slugs and worms.

Florence said that when her folks got word that her brother was missing in action, my grandmother kept doing her chores. She prayed while she worked. My grandfather disappeared into the cellar and stayed there for two days without eating.

God-land. I was raised in the land of believers. Strong true believers. All roads led to God. Every third sentence was directed His way. *Nothing lasts except belief. Rock of Ages. What a friend we have in Jesus.* Besides the Father, Son, and Holy Ghost, no other friends were worth having. Every night except Sundays, Florence would read from the Bible before bedtime. Lights out, and Florence, in her bathrobe, sat on the floor in the upstairs hallway, where my brothers and I, already in bed, could hear her voice. Trained in speech and dramatics, she would finish the scripture and then read a selection from the *Christian Missionary Alliance's Daily Devotional.* A sermonette. We took her perfect enunciation for granted. Her face cold-creamed, her hair pinned up, the Bible opened to the parable of Lazarus and the rich man. Lazarus, the beggar covered in sores, dies at the rich man's gate. On the same night, the rich man falls sick at his feast table and expires. The rich man is hurled into the flames of Hell, while Lazarus arrives in Paradise, carried in the bosom of Abraham. The rich man begs Abraham for one drop of water. He is denied. The thirst parable frightened me. I rolled from side to side, kicking my sheets. I tried praying. I heard only crickets. What was it like talking to God? Did my mother know how? Had she always? Why had she wanted to throw herself into the water as a girl? Had God stopped her? I wondered how you went about loving God. I wanted to love Him.

I thought of a picture I'd seen of my mother at my age. She wore a cotton shift and stood in a field, the cornstalks fighting it out on the ground behind her. The seams in her sleeves puckered and her hem bunched. Her hair blowing to the side, her thin dress, drab as a worn harness, lifted in the long-ago wind. I could smell manure hanging in the stillness, and I tried to hear what she was thinking. The girl, the one I wanted to know, like me, was waiting to step out of the cornfield, with its cool-as-moon sun. Did she love God then?

During that September visit, dementia had weakened God's hold on Florence. She said, "I wish I had read more from the Bible to you people growing up."

I tried to tell her that she had, but she shook her head back and forth. "Mom, we had Bible readings every night." Her head wagged adamantly.

No, no, no. Then she tried opening the newspaper to the obituaries again. I watched her. In the past, she read them line by line, but now she did little more than glance. No wonder the economic crisis of 2008 had passed her by. AIG tottering on the brink. Her securities were bound up in AIG, and the mother I'd been raised by would be alarmed at news of this crisis. Not a peep from her. I watched her start an article, but she wouldn't finish. She preferred tinkering in her desk with ballpoint pens that hadn't inked paper in decades. "There is not one interesting thing in your mother's house," Rob once said. Yet, to me, everything in her apartment was freighted with a thousand meanings; every physical object, a ghost. My father, Philip's, picture next to the blue glow of the swan vase. Philip's face young. I was already decades older than he when he died, yet he looked wise; his Christ eyes, dark brown and myopic, peering out into the remnants of his family.

Two days into my visit, I heard someone wailing my name. "Stephanie! Stephanie!" My neck stiff from sleeping on the couch, I opened my eyes. Florence stood naked in the doorway to her room. "Mom," I said. "What's wrong?" Her arms were crossed over her chest, but still you could see gravity pulling and emptying her breasts into bags of skin that had once been large and lovely. *How small she is growing,* I thought. "Stephanie, you're going to be mad at me." She reminded me of a little girl; her legs still good, but the muscles softened in her buttocks and her stomach cleaved by the scar from three Caesareans. An undertone of veins, blue, like fishhooks caught in her flesh. My blue and white mother's voice shook. "I was so cold in the bathroom. They took my heater. I turned the hot water on in the shower to warm things up." I jumped to my feet. The shower curtain had been removed by Village Ridge and not replaced, and the floor was flooded with water. I knelt in this lake and began sopping it up with towels. I called the office and, immediately, they sent up a maintenance man with a mop and a shower curtain.

"I'm so sorry," my mother said, dressed now.

"No problem, Florence," Garrett, the maintenance man, said, lifting his brows over piercing blue eyes, as if to say *Florence, you are a big damn problem.*

After he left, my mother said, "I don't trust him. He's funny." Like the funny weather. The winter tornadoes. The May snow.

Before my eyes, my diminished mother was devolving into the dementia mother and, yet, I didn't see it. Neither did my brothers. Her symptoms were a billboard for DEMENTIA. Her talking in her sleep, the music that she'd heard at night–hymns being sung in her ears, whole choirs, but she didn't mind the hymns. It was when the drum beat or the bass played *dum dum dum.* That, she couldn't stand. I noticed she had forgotten the names of her nieces and nephews. "Who is Uncle Fred's daughter?" "Do I spell *immediately* with one or two m's?" the former English teacher inquired. "Help me *right* a thank you to Amanda for her letter." The words stuttered coming out of her pen. Still, I did not think *dementia.*

Dementia was my great-uncle Frank, who lived with my great-aunt Anna on a small farm where we would go for Sunday dinner. My great-uncle, once a tinner at the meatpacking plant, sat in his jeans overalls, looking out his window into the red oak. *Dementia* was naked women twined into the fence along with the raspberry vines. Naked women in his trees, *eating his milk and drinking his eggs,* living in the chicken coop, and he had a mind to load his shotgun to scare them off. Aunt Anna cared for him. I can see him in the high-backed chair with stitched orange flowers, my brothers and I sitting at his feet, giggling. My mother told us to stop, that we were hurting Aunt Anna. Uncle Frank was her husband. That was *dementia.* What was called hardening of the arteries.

Big G

The more vulnerable my mother became, the better our relationship. My diminished mother was forgetting my long-ago crimes. The birth control pills in my patchouli-drenched army backpack. The newspapers she spread out on spring-break vacation so my clothes wouldn't touch the carpet. She was forgetting the jeans with holes, a rope for a belt. My dementia mother forgot that I'd been an uncontrollable teenager, that I had totaled her Rambler my senior year of high school, that I'd given away her movie camera and her 12-string guitar, that I'd been promiscuous.

My dementia mother did remember that after two Master's degrees, I hadn't settled into a career, but instead, worked endlessly at what she called my *dead-end job*; that I did not marry or produce grandchildren; and with my shadowy, precarious New York existence barely hanging on, no house into which I could offer her a home, as she and my aunt had my grandmother. I hoped that her mind had blurred the worst of my wild years; how, after graduating from high school, I announced that I was 18 and would do what I wanted.

⁂

Florence might have forgotten, but I hadn't, how her hands had gripped the Rambler's wheel. I slumped in the passenger's seat hungry for a cigarette as the green and gold of the Iowa countryside passed by. My mother was driving me to Central College's freshman orientation week in Pella, the same private college that my brother Brett attended. I'd given more thought to whether I'd eat a tenderloin or French fries at Uncle Milt's Drive-in than my choice of schools. Our destination lay another fifty miles west. Anger percolated inside me from last night's all-nighter. I'd tried methedrine for the first time with three friends and we talked until dawn in the Waubeek woods, a college send-off. In those days, methedrine was called *speed* or *crank.* Crank because of the crankiness or irritability you felt after the eight-hour high wore off. Now, coming down, I seethed and my mother had to suffer my presence. The terrible air.

"You ingrate, Stephanie; all that I've done for you and this is the way you act? Wearing those rags to meet your college roommate in," Florence said with a scowl. She wore a nylon dress, a sleeveless olive and brown shift, a necklace of gold links, and brown sandals with a half-inch heel. Her auburn hair no longer set in Betty Grable curls, but shorter, her bangs flat. "I've bought you beautiful clothes. Where are all those wonderful pantsuits?"

"I gave them away," I said, my lip curling. "No one wears pantsuits, they wear jeans."

"Yes, if they have nice ones. They don't wear them dirty with holes in the knees. I bought you an expensive jacket from Armstrong's and you threw it into your closet. You didn't have the courtesy to say thank you. Never in my life would I have dreamed I'd have such a thankless daughter."

The dark stove of my anger kept its heat turned up. I shook out a cigarette from my crumpled pack. Not once had I tried to smoke in front of her before.

"Oh, no, you're not!" she said, grabbing for the cigarette. "You're not smoking." Her eyes left the road and the car swerved toward the shoulder. I threw the unlit cigarette out the window.

I know that girl. I sense her ghost nearby–stifled, impulsive, reckless, selfish.

"I should disown you. Whoever heard of carrying a sleeping bag to college and no bedding, no sheets? I'm going to wash my hands of you."

"Wash your hands, then," I said, anxious to get away from my mother.

We drove into Pella, a sunny town where a Dutch community had taken root after forcing the Ioway and Chippewa tribes off the land. Once upon a time, this quiet town where the Tulip Festival was held in the spring would have charmed me. A Christian town that the youth-quake had not yet reached. Mom dropped me off in front of the Central College dorms and drove off. I sat cross-legged on the lawn, watching my dorm sisters and their parents lugging their suitcases in. Stewing in my own bad-tempered juices, I didn't want to think about my mother's disappointment.

After three weeks, I quit Central College. I left without withdrawing; I left without getting a tuition refund. A letter had come from Michael, the boy I'd met the summer before, who lived in a town outside Raleigh, North Carolina. *Drop by*, he wrote, if I was ever in his *neck of the woods*. I decided to hitchhike to North Carolina and visit him in his neck of the woods. It would be a surprise.

⁂

Outside Lynchburg, Virginia, the clouds came down and settled on the tops of the pines. I was only one state away, and then I would be in North Carolina. Rain slipped out of the pines and fell straight down in torrents. I stood by the roadside. Three cars splashed by, and then a van merged onto the interstate, the dusty white van from the truckstop café I'd passed. It stopped on the shoulder. The side door rolled open and a man in a red ball cap I recognized from the café shouted at me to hurry. There were three men in all. I hesitated.

"Come on," he shouted again.

Then I ran. No choice. I heaved my bag in and the man hoisted me up, rolling the door shut. "Sit anywhere," he offered, squatting over a toolbox. He took off his red cap, folding its bill and sliding it into his work overalls. No room because of all the cardboard and sawhorses and lunch boxes. I sat Indian-style on a wrench. The man stared at me hard, like he'd been asked to dig my grave in the rain and needed to know how much I weighed. I pulled my knees up to my chest and wrapped my arms around them. I was wearing a blue peasant blouse, blue jeans, and brown suede tie-up boots, as if the skins of antelope were wrapped around my ankles. My good-luck boots.

He ran his fingers through his oily dark brown hair. There were deep creases in his forehead. "I'm Billy," he announced, and cocked a thumb at the driver. "That's my boss, Big G."

Billy didn't introduce the man with blond hair, hunched in the passenger seat, who fidgeted with his silver cross. I noticed things. It was the one talent even my mother remarked on–curiosity, noticing. I wish I saw less; it would be quieter inside my head and my eyes wouldn't get so tired. What did I care if he wore a cross or fidgeted? He was the one who had stared at me the most in the café. Now he wouldn't look at me. Big G must have been in his fifties. His chin tripled when he smiled, and his head was gray as though shark flesh, with a blubbery blue eye set on the side.

The blond extended his hand over the seat. "I'm Junior."

I shook it and stared at a sample carpet scrap. Maroon was the shade of Mom's wine-colored velvet loveseat. Something floated between the men; a strain, a tension, as if they knew something I didn't, as if picking me up were something they'd made a bet on.

"So, how far are you going?" Billy nudged me with his knee, kicking the carpet sample aside.

"North Carolina," I said.

Big G lifted his blubbery eyes into the rearview again. "I'm only headed to Alexandria."

"That's good enough," I said. Alexandria was deeper into Virginia. That would put me closer to another state line.

Billy tapped my knee. "How old are you, Dark Eyes?" He tossed the empty Pepsi can into a sack. "Kind of pretty, ain't you?"

I had hitchhiked into the land of *ain't*. Men think they've given you something if they praise your looks. Once they've said you're pretty, they figure they have squatter's rights to you. Still, I felt a glow spread through me at hearing *dark eyes* and *pretty*. Mom had never told me I was pretty, although I'd heard her call my cousin's fiancée, JoLynn Gallup, beautiful; I'd heard her call Kay Erenberger from church beautiful. She remarked upon the beauties and the not-so-hots. Now I was sitting in the back of a van with men heading home from a construction job. I was the center of attention.

"How old?" he repeated.

"I'm 18."

"Eighteen," Billy snorted. "I'd put you at 16. Junior, you've got a girl who's 14. How does this one measure up?"

"You can't tell with girls. She could be 18."

"Where are you coming from?" Big G asked in the rearview.

"Iowa." I saw myself walking across campus with a backpack and my brother Brett, who had given me a ride to the highway. An act he would forever regret.

"Did you hitchhike all the way?"

"Through five states."

I saw myself hiking along the interstate, the reeds poking up from the ditches. The moon blazing bright as high noon on the green entrance ramps, cars whizzing past, the spill of their headlights over me, the red blinking of taillights. I saw a car pulling over, and me running to it, and just when I almost reached the passenger's door, it accelerated away, a game. Inside me, the farmhouse of my childhood, the place of light, was growing smaller and smaller. I was throwing myself into the big wild world now, after a childhood where nothing, nothing happened, and I wanted things to happen. I had never called Mom to tell her that I'd quit school; I had left that for my brother to do. My heart was set against my mother.

I pictured Florence returning from Hilda's Beauty Salon, the crunch of the Rambler's tires in gravel. I was 10, and had spent those hours of her absence scrubbing the farmhouse, its two stories, the huge thresher's kitchen, the living room, the family room, the mud room. Proudly, I stood in the sparkling clean kitchen, the woodwork sponged with warm vinegar, the carpets vacuumed, the floors washed, the bathtubs and sinks scrubbed. Wanting praise, wanting something, I shifted from one leg to another, and then Florence huffed, her hair freshly washed and set in its shellacked shoulder-length ringlets, and went straight to the corner table in the living room, where I'd stacked and made neat her papers and envelopes, the bills, the correspondence.

"I can never find anything after you clean," she said, sighing. "Where did you put everything?" She went to the sink, filled her red tin cup with cold water, drank, then stalked back to the corner table, spreading out all her papers that I'd straightened. "Where did you put my brown spiral notebook, Em?" When I irritated her most, she called me *Em*, short for *Emily*, my middle name. I told her I was running away. "Make sure you close the screen door behind you. I don't like flies coming inside." I bridled the donkey, Jack, and slowly rode down the hill toward Grandma's, where I spent the night. I had run away.

The van exited off the interstate. "Get down, keep your head down," Billy warned. We were dropping Billy and Junior off. Just before I ducked, I saw Big G sail the van into a subdivision. *Jesus is Lord of Wilderness Corners*, a sign read. Ranch houses. Cloth diapers snapping on a clothesline. The van wove between bumps in the asphalt road and came to a stop. I kept my head pressed to the maroon carpet scrap. The sound of boots, tools, and lunch buckets, then the van going again.

"Come up here." Big G patted the passenger's seat. "You can breathe easy now."

I pushed my bag up front, then climbed after it. Now I saw why he was called *Big G*. His girth pushed out his work shirt, and his green work trousers could have been harem pants, except they were packed with fat. My blouse still wet from the rain and the air conditioner blowing made me grow goose bumps. I started to shake.

"Angel, you're cold. There's a blanket in the back."

I noticed the gold band embedded in the flesh of his finger. "I'm fine," I told him through chattering teeth.

Big G reached back and dragged forward a fleecy blanket that gave off the odor of baby powder. He pulled it over my lap. "I have a daughter. I wouldn't let her out on the highway. I hardly let her get her driver's license. She's married now. She and my grandsons raise chickens. They have thousands of them things."

I felt warm, but Raleigh, North Carolina, was still a hundred miles away. There wouldn't be a field to sleep in like last night, and I wanted to curl up and sleep. Night was coming; where would I go? I'd thrown away college and my mother's money to do what? This?

Big G rattled the bag of barbecued pork rinds from the dashboard. The crispy purple rinds crunched in his mouth. "Tell you what I'm going to do. I'm going to get you a room. I know a place in Alexandria right off the highway. The Norlina Hotel."

I don't want to stay in a place he knows about, I thought. *I would owe him.*

Big G smoothed the blanket over my knees. "I'm a daddy. Little darling, you can't keep your eyes open. What kind of man would I be if I let you back out on the highway half asleep? I'm just going to turn the heater up." I could taste dust from the heater as Big G droned on about eggs. I knew exactly what he was talking about. "Those boys take them eggs and wipe off little blood specks without breaking a shell."

When I was 6 or 7, nothing was more frightening than being told to "Go pick the eggs." I feared inside the chicken coop, where the dark always gathered. Even when Mom or Grandma went with me, I cowered from the hens, with their wilted combs, their droppings hanging from the roosts like petrified spinach, the clucks and the stink, but most of all, I was afraid of reaching under the hen as she watched me with her yellow eye, ready to peck me as I snatched the egg. I was the monster there to steal and eat her child.

** **

Later, in the room that Big G had paid for, I picked up the phone. There was no dial tone. The front desk didn't answer either, and I was still holding the old black rotary telephone when Big G unlocked the door. My heart sank when I saw him and the KFC bag.

"MMMMM," he whistled. "Don't you look pretty. Why, your eyes are just so big. Witchy, aren't they?" He sat on the edge of the bed and unfolded a napkin. "Sit. We'll have a picnic."

We were in the mirror above the dresser like a couple at a church box supper. Big G lifted a tub of potato salad from the box. "I love potato salad, especially when it's fresh."

My toe rubbed at a bobby pin stuck in the rug. I picked at the potato salad. The potatoes were tough as chamois cloth. His lips smacked as I chewed, his jowls webbed with tiny red veins. Big G handed me a drumstick. "Eat some of this chicken. Do you know your cheeks don't have one pimple on them?"

After eating a few bites of the drumstick, I went to the sink to wash my hands. When I came back, Big G was still sitting on the edge of the bed, his pants puddled at his feet. He was jiggling his soggy penis–the harder he wiggled it, the soggier it got.

I pictured hens about to be butchered. How the whole coop started to cluck when Grandma went in with the gunnysack. Once the hen was inside the sack, she went still, because she knew. Grandma bundled the gunnysack to the chopping block and fit the hen's neck between two nails pounded into the stump. She lifted the ax and chopped its head off. The hen became an "it." You couldn't chop the head off a "her." Now I was inside the sack.

"Do you mind if I pet you some?" he asked, then took my hand in his. He wanted me to pet him. Tiny drops of sweat dotted his upper lip, and the skin sagged under his eyes, as if all the years of smiling had collected there. I let him move my hand. *It doesn't feel a thing,* I thought. His penis tried to sneak back inside him–tiny and lost, the hairs it nested in were frail and sticky–light brown and worn away.

"Squeeze it, please."

Warm vanilla pudding squished through my fingers.

For being such a sweet girl, Big G would come by in the morning and take me for breakfast at a place that served the best biscuits. Big G zipped himself. "I'll be here at 6:30."

⁂

I wandered through the room, touching the black telephone, the phone book five years old, the bath towel still wet, the light switch with a decal for Cold Spring ginger ale. I hugged a pillow to me. There were worse things: pulling hazel brush, eating cow tongue and rutabaga, Bev Kness yelling on the school bus, 'Hey, ugly Stephanie." I pulled the sheet over my head and closed my eyes. There stood Mom in her Red Cross uniform, with a soldier on either side of her, all three of them laughing, Mom's hand shading her eyes as if she were trying to see something way off in the distance. Trying to see her future.

Lightning flashed, and through the sheet I saw the room jump out of the dark–green, like Big G's uniform.

Thunder crashed, then rain. Heavy rain washing everything away.

Luther

On that September visit, the TV stayed off; the remote controls were Mount Everests for my mother's brain to climb. No reruns of *M*A*S*H* to brighten the house, no secretly enjoyed soap operas, and there was no inviting me to watch one of the fifteen taped sermons of D. James Kennedy, Ph.D., from the Coral Ridge Bible Hour. Other years, she would make a list of which sermons I'd viewed, and as she sat on the couch with the VCR remote in hand, she would watch me watching and repeatedly ask, "Is it loud enough? I can raise it if you like." The whole point was for me to hear, and her eyes hardly left my face. Like before meals on the farm when the prayer was being said in unison, Florence half-closed her eyes, and while her lashes flickered, she managed to see out and note if her children's eyes were properly shut. Those not-open/not-closed eyes, those inward- and outward-looking eyes, I was not to see again until the day her pre-active dying began.

Although my brother Brett was a sincere believer, my mother worried that Joel and I were not saved and, therefore, our family couldn't be reunited after death. Would we be perfected in the afterlife? Would our physical bodies come with us, and how would we get along? Better than here in Iowa? And where was this paradise place? Could it be the newly discovered bubbles of gamma rays on either side of our galaxy, 50,000 light years tall?

In September, there was no mention of saving grace. And while she took the names of the three men she'd married, I saw her slipping back into the name given her at birth–Florence Ruth Telecky. The name of her naked self. Likewise, her interests were winnowing down to the possessions she wanted to pass on. Her legacy.

"In my day, the children divided all their folks' household furnishings. I still have a cedar chest full of bedding and feather ticks and feather pillows. My grandmothers made them. I could never get you people to take anything."

But *her day* had been gone for ages. Having thought she'd die in the 20th Century, it was a new day she'd lived into. When my father died in 1957, she purchased her stone at the same time. *Florence Ruth Dickinson, 19__ to 19__.* She'd lived into the second decade of the 21st Century, the Internet age, the designer-baby age; she'd witnessed the human population on earth almost tripling. She'd been born to kerosene lamps and wood cookstoves and flat irons; her father had plowed with the workhorse's reins tied around his waist, and now there were biometrics and eye scans, wireless networks, and people of the same sex marrying. None of those things interested her any longer. The question of what to do with her wedding dress, lying all these years in the cedar chest, kept her awake at night.

I thought of the surviving video of my mother and father's wedding reception, held on my grandparents' farm. Grainy, spliced together, the old celluloid gave the viewer a sensation of being inside a snowstorm. Florence had bought a Super-80 movie camera and asked her cousin Edwin to capture the afternoon; the shaking of hands that no longer existed, except where the human ghosts talked and smiled. There was the summer kitchen and grape arbor, and my mother, shielding her bangs with one hand as she crossed the grass, the other hand hiking up the train of her gown, with its empire waist and sheer sleeves. The trees bending in a vanished wind and the cottony leaves flying up like fleece. I could see all the dear departed warming themselves in the July sun. Fields of snow corn growing in every direction.

Standing up from the breakfast table, she said, "Stephanie, I want you to look at my jewelry and take everything you can. I don't want you people throwing it all out after I'm gone. I know how you all are."

I followed her into the bedroom. She'd set out all her Fanny Farmer chocolate boxes, which once held caramels and now were receptacles for jewelry and cotton balls. She opened her gold-hasped wood jewelry box that her father had made, with its captured scent of nutmeg, perhaps a perfume that Florence had worn. "Honestly, all these beautiful beads. And jewelry dresses up everything." An array of circle beads rabbit-tailed with cotton balls, a vast assortment of clip-on earrings. Ruby Pear Cut Flowers with sets missing. Ritzy purple blobs. "Brett will throw everything away." Her jewelry. Her life, these beautiful, beautiful things. The only pieces I wanted were the heirlooms. The tangible proof of intangible love. The Black Hills gold necklace her parents had given her for high school graduation. The yoke of silver and gold leaves. The greenish-yellow seed pearl necklace given to her by Luther Worley. That single corn pearl in a slip of a chain worth infinitely more than any of it. The rest, costume pearls, an oyster bed of them. Potato pearls, double-stranded and single-stranded, pearls the color of buttermilk, and overcast, dark night pearls. This time, in order to please her, I began filling a box of jewelry to take with me. The dementia mother could be pleased, unlike the other, stronger, healthier one. I had failed her in so many ways. Here we were; she, delighted to be passing her treasures on. "I always wore these with my blue suit," Florence said. "I like beads you can wrap around your neck twice. I'm sorry you never married or had a home. I know I made mistakes. So many men proposed, and some of them are still alive."

I was surprised by her confessions, especially about the men in her life. My father, dead for so long, seemed more dream than real. Yes, she had been picky, waiting until 36 to marry, and in her day, that was old. My father had failed us all by dying. "If I had it to do over, I probably would have chosen differently."

Florence held the necklace Luther had given her. He had been her first love. The fine chain looped over a hand always large for a woman and now freckled with age spots. "This I'd rather you wore after I die. The rest you can take now." Such a delicate piece, a man who admired women's necks must have chosen it. Luther A. Worley. I've always been a little in love with him too. The dancer. First Lieutenant, U.S. Air Force. The pilot who went down with his crew into the Mediterranean Sea. Florence had given me a studio portrait of him, wearing his uniform as if he were born inside it, a cigarette between the fingers of his right hand. I can see the metal rope of a watchband on a tanned wrist. And the way his hand is casually extended at his hipline. Like a man who knows how to hold himself. The other hand in his pocket. The clear eyes and hint of a smile.

Florence sighed. "I could never have married Luther, because he couldn't hold a steady job. He wanted to open a movie theater. Then he decided not to. My father didn't like him. But, during the war, he joined the Air Force and became a pilot. He said he'd finally found what he wanted to do. He wanted to fly."

"So, if he'd survived the war and gotten a job as a pilot, you might have married him," I say, not really a question but a statement.

"Oh, Stephanie, I don't know. It was all so long ago."

And in the room of my mother's dying there is a yellowed newspaper article in a photo album–*Eastern Iowa Pilot Missing in War Theatre.* And a photo. Handsome in that way Czech men are; sculpted faces and blue eyes, slender, and with a strange shyness.

Luther A. Worley on Iowa honor rolls of the dead. He seemed to be one of the few men in Florence's life whom dementia had not tarnished. "I think he really loved me," she told me as we waded through the endless necklaces, more boxes in her bottom dresser drawer, her closet, underneath bookshelves. "Yes, he truly was in love with me. Once, we went to a dance and there was a girl there who liked Luther. She always spoke to him. I told Luther it was that girl or me, and he never spoke to her again." He was three years younger than her. She loved to dance and he was a wonderful dancer. She loved to sing and he sang. He played the piano, the violin. He was beautiful to look upon.

"Daddy was different from Luther," she said.

My father was of English descent. After the war, my mother found herself in Reno, Nevada, teaching math. Florence the Iowa girl was at a church bonfire, a hotdog roast with Bible discussion, and she heard a man ask such an intelligent question she looked to see who he was. Such chance meetings determine genetic inheritance. She talked of his Harley-Davidson, and how she rode behind him through the deserts of Nevada and up the Pacific Coast Highway to Oregon, but she never spoke of dancing with my father. And it is only now, in this moment when I can no longer ask her anything, that I wish to know the answer to the question I never asked. *Did you love him?*

Perhaps my father had not loved her in the way that Luther had. He was a man's man, a sportsman. He didn't give her seed pearls and tell her she had his heart. My father liked his male friends, his hunting trips. He referred to my mother as "the wife." In the last-known letter that he had written to a co-worker at the State of Illinois Wildlife Commission, he tells his friend that he will have heart surgery, and his recovery, the doctors have told him, will take about a month. The car belonging to the State of Illinois needs to be picked up, or "the wife" can deliver it. And, then, as if some portent washes over him, he tells his friend how much he has enjoyed working with him the past two years.

⁂

Dementia. It consumes. In the last month and a half of her life, Florence's dementia, which had been an undertone, a current in the stream of her personality, became full-blown. It flowered. The woman who always covered herself with clothing, who wore a safety pin at the throat of her nightgown and could not stand to look at the exposed skin of others, who said to me again and again, "Cover up. I don't want to see your breasts"; this woman began to undress in front of others.

Why, when she took to her last bed, did she strip her clothes off? Because she wanted to get between the sheets and was too lost to find her pajamas? Or was it animal instinct? Maybe she lay naked in her bed because she had been tired a long time and needed to rest, and she could not do that in her stretch pants and sweater. Although she was among strangers, in her last weeks my reserved mother hugged and wanted to be touched; she held onto the hands of her favorite aides. Other aides she resisted, and stamped her feet when they tried to touch her.

In frontotemporal dementia, there are extreme personality changes. But my mother never truly seemed to be someone else, naked or clothed, making nice or being nasty. Ever the spirited farm pony, she didn't curse, although she had a storehouse of guttural expressions from the farm to express crudity. "You're full of prunes," the least of them. The dementia mother had asked my brother who the woman sitting at the edge of the bed was. Brett had said, "There's no one there, Mom." I would have asked a question: "What does she look like?"

The mother who banked annuities did not buy herself new underwear. She wore mid- thigh cotton briefs filled with holes, their elastic worn out. When she was being assisted with her morning dressing, aides noticed her wretched underthings, and informed my brothers. For all her closets filled with pantsuits and dresses–many of them expensive gifts from my wealthier, fashion-conscious Aunt Patsy–there was nothing for the intimate flesh. Or was that the disgusting primitive thing–the crotch. Moths of age ate equally into her flesh, her brain, and her underwear. She had hoped the tattered panties would see her through and, so, marooned in her last years in the retirement village without her car friend, she was left to shroud her privates in rags and safety pins. Two years ago, when Rob came with me to Iowa, we had taken Florence to Kmart to look for underwear. And there, amid the wilderness of nylon tricot, black and pink and cream and white bikini panties, we searched for simple cotton briefs for an elderly woman whose first underwear had been homemade bloomers that buttoned in back. They were not to be had. "There's nothing for me here," she said. "Buy something for yourself." She fished in her billfold (never a *wallet* to her) for her MasterCard.

Dementia is my mother's caught voice on my home answering machine. Wanting to say, "This is your mother," instead what comes out is, "Is your mother there? Where is your mother?" *Dementia* is Florence going down to the cafeteria for breakfast in the middle of the night. *Is your mother there?* And where am I? Her daughter. I am at work in New York City. Writing by night, and by day correcting financial statements, I had boxed myself in. There are a thousand roads I could have taken that would not have led here.

And for that life I stayed in New York City, while my mother wandered the night halls of Village Ridge, looking for the farmhouse.

Yes, where was Florence's daughter? That morning, this morning, any midmorning? Getting to the cubicle's enclosed area. That morning, this morning. I am setting my purse down, draping my jacket from chair back, pressing the ON button of my computer, taking out a Vitamin Pak, cutting into the Pak with scissors, opening my bottled water, swallowing vitamins: multi, E, C, fish oil; watching Windows and Citrix programs blink to life. I'm sweaty from the infernal dash to work, wishing I could invent a people wash (like a car wash), a step-through spritzer that scrubs you and blows clothes back on you. My face bathed in the blue screen, I reach out. The in-box is filled with a pile to be plowed through. There I sit. Sat. Twenty years evaporated.

Dementia. Delirium. I am rereading a letter Florence wrote me in March that shows everything being stripped from her, except the ability to care for children. Dementia, I've read, often blunts the emotions of the sufferer. But, until the last month of her life, her care for her children seemed to grow stronger. "My memory is so poor. The hour just past disolves." She misspells the word *dissolves* "disolves." But she only misses it by one letter. There are jumps in her logic, but I understand what it is she's trying to say across this gulf. This great "disolve" of personhood.

Seahorses Riding Black Waves

Florence hadn't forgotten that I had been shot when I was 18. That I'd hitchhiked for the second time to North Carolina to meet my boyfriend without telling anyone. That we went to a party and my boyfriend's best friend shot me–drunkenly, accidentally–paralyzing my left arm. I know now what a tragedy that was to her. Then, I selfishly thought that I alone bore the burden.

Few remember me before the shooting, how I looked before I impulsively made the mistake that would haunt me for years to come. I had hitchhiking in mind when my friend Cynthia drove me to the interstate, where I would head east toward Pennsylvania. I planned to meet my boyfriend, Michael Weston, at the Allentown Greyhound bus depot, and we would thumb together to Cary, North Carolina. His best friend, Charlie, was throwing a Thanksgiving Day party and we were invited. What was I thinking, sneaking away without telling my mother where I was going? Do you think of consequences when you are 18? No! Trembling, afraid of hitching alone although I'd done it before, I stuck out my thumb. Getting into a stranger's car felt like walking on the surface of Mars. A car pulled over and I was on my way.

⁂

A blizzard had been forecast for the Midwest, and in the middle of Indiana, it started to snow. Perhaps the forecast was a sign that I should have canceled the Thanksgiving date. A pale-blue Volkswagen, already crowded, stopped. They said they could take me to Cleveland. In front, the bucket seats were filled with the driver, his wife, and their infant son, and in back, two long-haired guys and their overstuffed backpacks. One of the guys was wearing wire-rimmed glasses and a red jacket, and I sat on his lap. My hair was short then, and his soft beard tickled the side of my neck. The blizzard began in earnest, and the VW shuddered and swerved, but the driver managed to keep us on the road despite the blinding snow and wind. I've forgotten so much of that trip but not the body warmth inside that bubble of a car, as if we occupied a diving bell in a frenzied sea of snow.

Another ride took me from Cleveland to Allentown, where I planned to meet Michael. The bus depot was about to close, and he was nowhere to be found. A police officer approached me. "Are you Stephanie?" I thought I was about to be arrested. He told me that Michael was in jail, and then he laughed. The police officer had offered him a cell to sleep in and said I could sleep there too. He would give us a ride to the interstate in the morning. Now there was no shielding me from that headline: IOWA GIRL SHOT IN CARY. I am sure the policeman couldn't fathom kids hitchhiking in the middle of the night; he was horrified by it.

I am hitchhiking in some corner of my mind at all times–the dread and thrill of the dark, the vehicle pulling over, and all you know of him (it was always a *him* driving, and sometimes a *her* with him) is his taillights. The door opening and "How far are you going?" his question or yours. My generation was testing out the Interstate Highway System. And some of us paid dearly for it.

⁂

Cindy Street. The most innocuous of street signs pointed the way to Charlie's house, to the Thanksgiving bash that Michael's friend had invited us to, and was throwing to celebrate his parents being in France.

"Are Charlie's parents rich?" I asked Michael. I couldn't picture my mother or any of my friends' mothers and fathers spending the money to venture that far from home.

He wiped his mouth after drinking from his fifth of Boone's Farm Apple Wine. We'd just walked through the cemetery, where the late afternoon haze lingered over the toppled stones and blade-scratched slave names. *Jeer. Gazetta. Cuff. Accessory.* The leaves of the swamp oaks and honeylocust still whispered the secrets of long-ago lynchings.

"Charlie's mama is from Paris. She met Marshall Dunham, a swaggering U.S. Army sergeant, during the Liberation of France. He fixed her up with an extra ration card or some such thing. Every year they visit her folks in *Gay Paree*, but this is the first year that old Charlie gets to stay on his own. The house has been entrusted to him for a solid week."

The dusking light sifted through the air, and he squeezed my hand with his long, pale fingers. I wondered if Michael and Charlie's friendship had cooled since early October and that night in Chapel Hill. The night the eight-track had played itself through and began for the third time. Syllable after syllable. The night Charlie had flirted with me, asking Michael if he could have sex with me.

"Are you going to let him kiss you?" Michael asked.

"No, not even if you ask me to."

"Count on it, honey," he said. "I'm not going to ask him to." I looked up and saw the soft ferocity in his Black Irish eyes, the blighted potato fields and famine boats of his forebears. We hugged like we were one being broken into two halves.

I forgave him for telling me if I ever got pregnant to forget his name. I forgave him for informing me after his sister's wedding, "I'm not going to be only with you." I forgave him for the Thanksgiving dinner served at his house being a far cry from the Thanksgiving feasts of my childhood. His mother's turkey looked ill-treated even before her husband started to carve, the steak knife squeaking through the breast meat. On my plate the turkey had puddled in its watery sweat, while my fork picked at dry stuffing, instant mashed potatoes, and canned creamed corn. Yet I liked his open-minded parents, who let their son's girlfriend sleep on their couch and eat at their table. I liked his parents because they acknowledged that I was the only one of Michael's chums who helped wash the dishes.

"Ma's meat made me a vegetarian," Michael secretly admitted. "Her cooking is why Dad lives on black coffee and cigarettes."

Still, I missed my grandmother's farm on Thanksgiving, where the Buresh and Telecky clans gathered, the counter crowded with platters sizzling from the oven. The twenty-pound turkey stuffed with fragrant bread and roasted to a perfect pitch of tenderness. Uncle Douglas showing off his new electric knife, the blade traveling through the fowl's juicy flesh as though gliding through butter, then his electric knife moving on to cavort with the ham, the chicken, and the roast beef. A food orchestra. Sauerkraut and dumplings, sweet potatoes, cucumber and cabbage salads, homemade pickles, and homemade rye bread all had their solos. At the end of the U-shaped counter, the pies–apple, mince, pecan, pumpkin, rhubarb, and the cream pies–coconut, lemon, banana–their meringues so stiff and light they looked like lost clouds.

Michael and I held hands. The November moon had started to come up, a pale shaving with mist around it. The air crisp like bitten-into apple, with just enough of a chill to tell you it was autumn. "Check out the jackrabbit there on the moon," he said, peering up. "All you can see tonight is his ear. Right there where the craters are, do you see?"

"I think so," I blushed, delighted by the little-boy look on his face but ashamed to tell him about my nearsighted eyes, how impossible it was for me to see distance without my glasses. I had snugged my wire-rims into the army-surplus shell carrier I used for a purse; the case fit.

I expected Charlie's street to be nicer than Michael's, and it was. People who made good money lived on Cindy Street and people who made no money lived on Normandy. Instead of junk cars, bird feeders threw blue shadows on the well-kept lawns, and each house had its own deck and double garage. The black walnut and tulip trees watched us stroll past as if we were thieves.

"It's the next one," he said, pointing to a handsome two-story house with only one car parked in the driveway–Charlie's white Toyota. "Hey, what's that?" he asked. I'm not sure I answered his question. Actually, I didn't remember until Michael reminded me how the house seemed bathed in a flickering redness, the redness of an aura pulsating around the edges of the house and over the roof. The red light seeped even from the panels of the garage doors.

"Do you think we should go in?" he asked.

I shrugged. How could we not; we were already there.

Charlie hit the garage door OPEN button and stood in the space filled with only one vehicle. He grinned and waved us in. "Hey, come on." His side-parted hair swept his shoulders and swooped across his forehead. His blue jeans sported creases and his T-shirt looked as if his French mother had pressed it. I turned away from the grin that crinkled up his squishy blue eyes. Not even cousin to a smile, Charlie's grin didn't seem aimed at anyone in particular; it just stayed there as if it were his only expression and meant nothing, or else he was enjoying playing a private joke on us all.

"Hey, Michael, are you thirsty? I pulled every bottle out from the old man's liquor cabinet," Charlie said, flipping his hair out of his eyes.

I followed them into the kitchen, where copper pots hung over a marooned stove island. A pumpkin basket stuffed with Indian corn sat on the maple table. I could see the ceiling fan turning in the wood between the bottles. Jack Daniel's, Cutty Sark, Jim Beam. Beers. More fifths of Boone's Farm Wine. It was still early, but Charlie had started drinking his own Thanksgiving feast.

"Where is everyone?" Michael asked. "Where's Janet?"

"Janet's in Charlotte with relatives. Her sister's going to be here." Charlie brushed a grocery sack off a chair next to where he stood. "Hey, Iowa girl, you can sit here." I stayed standing. Across the forest of bottles, a moon-faced blond guy sat in the early-Americana chair drinking Jim Beam, his eyelids like lowered flags. "This fella here is another Charlie," Charlie said, then wished us all a Happy Thanksgiving and hiccupped. "Michael, drink up. Let's get liquored." The two Charlies, both long-hairs, were slurring, already drunk. *Long-hairs* was how we distinguished between the short-haired rednecks and the long-haired *freaks*. We proudly called ourselves freaks. I didn't know that this kitchen, with the basket of Indian corn on the table, surrounded by a whiskey forest of bottles, would be the antechamber to true freak-hood.

From my vantage point here in the 21st century, I'm trying to see myself through all that distance. Still suspended in the 1970s, I hardly recognize my younger self in Charlie's kitchen, taking off my Army/Navy coat. Underneath I'm wearing blue jeans and a blue-and-orange puff-sleeved peasant top as if a bird-of-paradise; I'm slipping out of it with two arms, two beautiful hands; I don't have to hold the sleeve below my clenched fist; not self-conscious of who may be looking at my forearm and hand stiffened at my elbow's end like a freeze-dried channel catfish. Rigor mortis.

Michael hovered over me, reaching for a beer. He filled a glass with Boone's Farm Wild Cherry Wine for me, so sweet it tasted like perfume or an apple turnover.

"Drink it. Have another," Charlie said.

I drank, then moved away from the table. Between sips, the grain in the wood held my face. When I looked up, the kitchen seemed longer, thinner. "Can I have some water?"

"Be my guest."

Charlie opened the cupboard. Inside were chunky ruby goblets with clusters of grapes. I filled a glass. I stared out the window into the growing dark, waiting for my head to clear.

His hand slipped around my waist and I moved away, not wanting to stumble into something. There were crabapple trees out back, and I could see their dry leaves shaking.

⁂

So I am returning to Cary, North Carolina, and Charlie Dunham's parents' house, to the Thanksgiving Day party, to the table crowded with liquor bottles. Charlie's house reminded me of my aunt and uncle's on Country Club Drive; instead of the sunken living room and cathedral ceiling, here the carpets were a pearl blue, and pale-blue curtains billowed in the window, so sheer the night air might tear them. I wanted to look at myself in the mirror to brush my hair.

Charlie guided me down the hall, laughing. "Hey, honey," he slurred. "You came all the way from Iowa and you're not going to give me a kiss?" How do I know those were his exact words? I can still see his light brown hair side-parted in the way Southern males combed their long locks, that sheet of hair falling in his blue eyes, and always the laugh, his smile that seemed to be hiding a sneer. I can count on my hand the number of times I saw him, but there isn't a day since that Thanksgiving that I haven't felt his presence intensely. He has never left my side.

"I can't kiss you," I said, or maybe I smiled and stayed quiet. I know that a part of me had been excited by his attention. His brutality. Now I can admit that.

The hallway he pointed to was darkened, and you could feel the parents being gone, taking the watchfulness with them. I walked over the blue carpet in my brown suede ankle boots to the bathroom, feeling above the sink for the light switch. It was cooler in here, away from the bottles. I patted my way over the wall. Where was the switch? I didn't have to pee, so I left the door open. In the light from the kitchen, the shower curtain with seahorses riding black waves came to life. The toilet seat cover was swaddled in blue fur. I looked at the glasses on the sink and the toothbrush holders without toothbrushes. There wasn't real music in this house. If I had found the light switch, I might have saved myself. Lights on, I would have closed and locked the bathroom door.

I wonder now if I am remembering my remembering of the shooting. My body reacts when I hear a sharp sound like a manhole cover lifting as a truck rolls over it and then drops it–BANG. I flinch, startled, my heart races, and I bolt out of the way. In my flesh there is no remembering necessary, as the shooting exists outside of chronological time. It is embodied in the ever-ongoing present. Now I am my older self and must again press the towels to my nose and breathe in the odor of dewberry soap and the reek of money. I'll stand in the semi-dark of the bathroom, seeking but not stumbling upon the light switch. When I find my face in the semi-dark mirror staring wide-eyed, I resurrect my younger face with the round smooth cheeks and no scar. The scars I've grown so used to not yet there. I might be pretty enough.

I saw Michael in the mirror behind me and I turned to him.

"I want to talk to you," he said, his face pale. "I think we should leave."

He didn't crouch down but stayed standing. It was I who sat on the plush toilet lid's blue fur cover. It has been important to me in telling the story to make sure the listener understands that I wasn't going to the bathroom. As the years pass, I tell the story less and less. It is an old war wound few are interested in.

"Why?" I asked.

"Charlie has gotten out his father's shotgun. Things are getting out of hand."

Was I thinking, before Michael swept in, how quiet and pale blue and nice the bathroom was? My left hand does not know these are the last minutes of its life.

In *Half Girl*, my autobiographical novel about the shooting, I put words in Michael's mouth, words he would never have been so unhip as to kneel in front of me and utter. "Darling, darling, you know I like you better than any *chick* I ever met in my life. You've got a mind." Yes, he'd told me I had a mind, that my eyes were large and mysterious, beautiful eyes, but never would he have lifted my boot and kissed it. And he never said those words that I put in his mouth. "I am scared shitless I might love you." Yet he had thought them, he'd admitted years after the fact, long after they had potency, long after our time had passed. He had wanted us to be together, a couple, but instead he'd said, "I'm not going to ball just you."

Still, I liked his house, with the holes in the plywood, with the doors off their hinges; his harried yet generous parents, who'd been set down in a North Carolina town, a bedroom community for IBM workers, and were trying to make the best of it; who didn't have much but shared even the food on their table. I preferred Michael's failings to Charlie's, his trying to appear more sinister than he was.

There wasn't time for love words or thoughts. Not even a minute after Michael said we should go, the bathroom door flew open.

"Y'all took off on me," Charlie said, slurring. His hair hung in his eyes.

"Hey, put that thing away," Michael said.

Charlie held a shotgun and balanced it on his right hip. One of the 12-gauge shotguns that came from his father's gun cabinet, a cabinet that blended in with the furniture. Now it didn't look like a bookcase or buffet. One of Charlie's friends had come into the bathroom. His name happened to be Paul, and I'd forgotten him standing in the tub near the showerhead, giggly with the excitement of being in the presence of a loaded gun. And the other Charlie stood behind Charlie, looking in over his shoulder.

"Is that thing loaded? It might go off, you know," Michael said.

Charlie shuffled a few more feet into the bathroom. Behind him the hall light was shining, the sconce lamp making a halo around his head.

Later, when I wrote a fictional treatment of the shooting in *Half Girl*, I believed, yes, that my life had led me here: Mom, who loved me but disliked me too; my father, who had died; the religion that went in one of my ears and out the other; my oldest brother who shot BBs into the donkey's behind when I rode him; my middle brother, who hammered open Grandpa's musket on the anvil, making the grit and buckshot remains explode against my legs; the neighbor boys always shooting, shooting at anything that flew.

"Why'd y'all take off on me?" he asked a second time. "We're just starting to party. I was looking and thought y'all might have gone home."

I listened to his sentences. To his *y'all's.* The words Charlie used were so simple, you'd hardly notice them in a conversation, but with the shotgun on his hip, every word seemed heavy with meaning behind the words, not in front.

He slowly shook his head and laughed. The gun looked funny in the bathroom. Was that why he kept laughing? The barrel dipped and wove. Where was his hand? I needed to see where his finger was.

"Charlie, please put the gun away. You're scaring me," I said.

No warning, no sirens, no squeal of tires in the street. Nothing. No time. Ghosts of pheasants and elk sprinted and bucked against the walls.

I heard a roar like a steel plate lifting and falling in the street. Blue flames exploded from the barrel of the gun. The flames felt as if they were in the air a long time, but it must not have been long at all. I didn't have time to even raise my hands. The blue flames hit my face. It felt like a skillet of hot grease. *This is what happens in the newspapers.* I wanted to laugh. It was happening to me and there was no going back. The buckshot hit my left cheek with such force it lifted me up, raising me above the tub. I could feel pieces flying out of me, like corn spattering from a sheller. Hard bits. I was opening up. God, I couldn't breathe. I was straddling the blue flame. Then it dropped me.

Charlie yelled, and Michael screamed, "Oh my God, God."

The house vanished into an enormous black. I must have toppled onto the floor, because I could hear their voices above me, but I couldn't see them. My eyesight was gone; I couldn't find my arms or legs. I was lost inside my own body. I gasped for air. It felt like someone was holding a hand over my mouth and pinching my nose closed, but it was my own blood I must have been swallowing. The gun went off. I was lifted up, pellets breaking my jaw, teeth flying, a hole blown into my cheek. All that, I learned later.

At that moment, there were no thoughts; I was all animal, unable to breathe, trying to crawl outside to get air, to die.

The grinning boy had changed the whole trajectory of my life. Soon I would hardly have a body; I would become a *burning*. What a Thanksgiving it must have been for my mother, to get the phone call from Duke University Hospital telling her that her daughter had been shot, and asking for permission to operate.

⁂

They knew my name. "Let's bear down, Stephanie," the nurses told me when something hot or sharp was about to happen. One put a pen into my hand; another held a notepad under it. "Is your name Stephanie?" I flew in morphine dreams, flying through clouds that scratched themselves on the top branches of giant white oaks, flying into swollen suns, climbing ladders tall as skyscrapers, swinging from ropes in an outer-space hayloft. Then, always, I would fall, slipping from ladders and ropes, flying among the stars; then endlessly dropping through space. The falling would land me back on Cindy Street, under the full moon, with its light so pale but concentrated, Michael and I debating whether to go into Charlie's house. What can I say now to the woman who is wordless but gave me my corporeal self; who watched me throw it away, then fought to save what remained. I floated with brightness around me, as if my pores were fireflies that had just birthed. I heard the muffled hoot of an owl and wondered if I had died.

For a month I lay in a hospital bed, on a catheter, left arm splinted to a board, jaw wired, my lungs filigreed with shrapnel, trying to breathe with a respirator until I was able to breathe on my own. This is where my thumb and the friendly blue Volkswagen had taken me.

Into the fiery embrace of a shotgun.

Eden

Joel is making us a midnight supper in the rental studio, though it is 11:00 p.m. I listen to him in the kitchen; his banging around in the cupboards sounds like our mother. We speak of our mother's loneliness. The fireflies are still below in the parking lot, sparking the dark.

My brother serves me tuna steak and pickled cabbage and Hy-Vee kale salad. He stands at the counter, cutting his fish. "I'm not sure Mom would have been any happier if she had lived close to one of her children than she was here," he says, spearing tuna on his fork. "She'd still have to deal with old age and isolation. When Mom still lived in her apartment, she kept to herself. Did you ever meet any other women here like her? She'd smile, but never invite anyone to her apartment. Never visit anyone else. Never call a friend. They'd have little parties here, but she claimed she couldn't hear. She preferred being alone, looking through her clippings. Or hiding her dentures in a sock and burying it in the closet, where no one could find them without tearing the whole place apart."

I stare at my plate, unable to eat the fish or the Hy-Vee potato salad. Everything, from the pickled purple cabbage to the fish, is either sour or raw. I envision my mother in her loneliness. Her empty dignity. "I was a teacher. I am not a child." She was insulted by the birthday parties, the sing-alongs, and bingo. The prongs of my plastic fork wear my lipstick. Now all the grievances I've carried are being squirreled away. "Why do you wear that orange lipstick? Do you want people to think 'Here Comes Lips?'" "Your hair looks like straw. Why don't you let me cut those dead, ragged ends?" "How can you go with that Bill Boyle after your friend Cynthia dumped him? I would never accept another woman's leavings." "You don't think; you just *do do* in a hurry." "I showed your poem to my friend who teaches Robert Browning at Coe. She said this is a series of impressions. She didn't even finish reading it." Now those grievances are being hauled to the dumpster. And what of the letters that used to come, page after page of her talking until she was blue in the face, all the good advice in one ear and out the other? I never took one suggestion she ever gave me. Not one.

Joel finishes eating and takes my plate to the sink. He understands why it's hardly touched. We speak of loves, won and lost. My ex-boyfriend with anger issues; my present partner, Rob, a brilliant visionary poet with Asperger's syndrome. Only Brett can boast a long-lived marriage, which produced two beautiful children, Amanda and Seth.

Joel tells me how he flew with Florence from Cedar Rapids to Dallas for our niece's wedding; she had balked at first and refused to pack. After the ceremony and the reception, they'd shared a motel room with double beds. Our mother had cried out in her sleep; she lashed out at her demons. It was her last trip.

* *

Hers was a life marked for suffering. After Joel's birth, post-partum depression swallowed her. Instead of joy, she felt suicidal. Joel turned out to be a colicky baby. Nothing seemed to stop his crying. Instead of nurturing, she felt murderous.

"Everything was black," she'd admitted. "You feel like you want to hurt someone." She never expressed exactly who that someone was. Herself? Her baby? Like all of my mother's stories, they were repeated endlessly. She seemed not to remember, nor care, whether her daughter or sons had heard them before. Her children were treated with the same disregard as she treated herself.

During the worst of her post-partum depression, my mother and Joel went to recuperate at my grandparents' farm. With its pastures and roaming chickens, its salads of loose leaf lettuce from the garden, its milk from the cow, the summer farm was Eden. "My father took the pills the pediatrician prescribed," Florence told me time and time again, a note of triumph in her voice. "He got his shovel, dug a hole behind the barn, and buried them. That's what he thought of those dumb pills." He believed the pills had made his daughter sick. They were alien, city pills. You burned or buried garbage on a farm, and my mother's nerve pills were garbage. Florence retold that story hundreds of times. To her, it showed her father's wisdom and caring. To me, it seemed frightening. It revealed that her father, and not her husband, had been the one most concerned about her. My grandfather drove my mother to the family doctor, a Czech man. "Dr. Smurha put me on iron pills and told me to get pregnant again. That's why the boys are so close in age." The depression lifted. But, in her 90s, the blackness returned with a vengeance.

Obsession had characterized her last six-and-a-half years, and seemed to drive out all delight and remembrance of past pleasures. Her two brothers and one sister hadn't endured the death of a fiancé, the death of two husbands, the shooting of a daughter, and the raising of children alone. They'd had astonishingly long marriages and successful professional lives. Some had even become wealthy.

⁂

I am sure before dementia swept clean the shelves of her short-term memory, Florence could summon up the day I flew home to Iowa from North Carolina. When she met me at the airport, I was no longer the daughter she'd given birth to, but the girl the shotgun had brought into the world. I, too, find it hard to return to the late January afternoon when I tottered out of Duke University Hospital. The sky was gray and the sun pale, not much brighter than a candle flame. You could see by its light, but not feel its heat. The outside had changed since Thanksgiving. Magnolia trees stood without leaves, but you could smell pieces of them. The chill, all the solemnity, suited me. Michael's mother drove us to the Delta gate of the Raleigh–Durham Airport. My legs shook and I held onto Michael's arm. His black hair trailed down his back and his skin looked pale, as if the shooting had happened to him too. The last time I'd walked beside Michael it had been Thanksgiving. From his mother's kitchen I carried the platter of dry turkey. The cornbread stuffing that almost rattled inside the bird's gut. Had that afternoon been drenched in foreboding, or had we both made that up? Hindsight?

"I'm not ashamed of you, honey," he said. "I should have protected you better." Did I imagine that he leaned in to get a better look at my neck? A zigzag of black X's. The X's marked scar rivers and tributaries. He brushed the hair away from the left side of my face, which gauze bandages covered. "These are your souvenirs. You paid a high price for knowing me." He kissed me goodbye. "We'll be together again," he said. But we wouldn't be together again, since together we'd called down a calamity.

⁂

The flight attendant asked for my boarding pass. After I handed it to her, I showed her the scissors that hung from a strap around my neck and explained between clenched teeth that my jaw was wired together. If I happened to get airsick, the wires would need to be cut. A waterfall of jet black hair cascaded to her waist; I'd never seen anyone so beautiful, nor felt so ugly.

It was my first time flying. The plane took off and we rose into the violent air over the heartland hitting turbulence–winter storms riding the upper reaches of the atmosphere. The cabin went black and winds shook the plane, the wings tilting from side to side. I liked the rocking, the jostling, the bumps. I was turbulence too–unsettled, chaotic. I would be for years.

We landed on the Cedar Rapids runway in the falling snow. My bag felt heavy, although it was only half-filled, with hospital slippers, Kleenex, and the red transistor radio Florence had bought to keep me company. Wobbling, I started down the ramp. I'd returned from the land of the almost-dead with my lifeless left arm in a sling, Michael's mother's black jacket draped over my crooked shoulders, and his sister's too-big jeans on my leaf-thin body. On my feet, the brown ankle boots, my "lucky" boots, the suede stiffened with blood. The boots were the lone survivors of the shooting; my jeans and sweater had been cut off me and thrown into the hospital incinerator.

I struggled down the ramp into the airport waiting area, where people crowded together, waving to and greeting their arriving passengers. Florence, in her black-and-white coat, stayed apart. Under the coat she wore a brown skirt, her teaching clothes. It must have been a weekday. In the hospital, I'd lost track of the days.

I took a deep breath. Which Mom would she be? There were two Florences, two mothers, the warm one and the angry, hard-to-please one. The Florence who visited in the hospital and listened while the respirator took its deep breaths in my body, who watched the nurses insert the skinny tubes into the tracheotomy site and suction out the phlegm, had been the warm mother. The mother so understanding and intelligent you felt immersed in a gentle cooling bath. The warm mother had witnessed the doctor at Duke taking off his glasses before approaching me and peeling the bandages from my cheek. "Oh, my," she'd said, "look at what that ugly kid did to her beautiful face." She'd startled at the Q-tips with handles long as Dairy Queen malt spoons used to swab the cheek wound and then the neck. The doctor bent over me. "We're debriding her cheek and removing pieces of buckshot. We'll get as many off as we can before we close the wound." He held up long tweezers with pointed tips so fine they could pick up dust. I could see bits of shot. She had said "her *beautiful* face."

Everyone loved the warm mother, *everyone*, especially her children. Responsibilities I can only guess at must have weighed on her, and the critical mother often was in charge. Then you forgot the understanding mother, could hardly fathom her existence, one Florence so completely blotted out the other.

Seeing me now at the airport, she neither smiled nor opened her arms to hug me. She pointed to seating near the gift shop filled with Hawkeye State knickknacks. "Go on, use the restroom."

I was hardly sure my feverish body could keep walking.

In the ladies' room, the woman at the next sink watched me; her curious, not unkindly eyes met mine in the mirror. I wanted to hide myself. The water faucet required you to press down on the *hot* or *cold* while you washed one hand and then the other. No twist or lever you could turn on to keep the water falling. I hit the water with my right hand and hurried to wash it under the stream for a second before it stopped. I refused to see what she saw, what everyone could see. The droop in my lip, the difference in my eyes; the left one dilated, the right a pinpoint. Melted snowdrops. A disfigured daughter.

Florence led the way through the parking lot to the blue Rambler. Her face looked expressionless and frozen, like a farm implement left in the snow. "You don't have a scarf on and that coat isn't warm enough," she said, taking off her red wool scarf and wrapping it around me.

I skated across the ice after her. The red wool scarf that she had knotted under my chin itched. I lifted my face into the falling snow, each flake stinging like a tiny sickle. She unlocked the trunk, and my duffel bag joined the spare tire, the RC Cola returnable bottles, and the bucket of sand there, in case we needed traction.

Settling herself behind the wheel, she snapped on her seat belt and found another scarf for herself stuffed in the crease between the seats. Her hands fit the key into the ignition. "What did the doctors say about your arm?" she asked, letting out a sigh.

"They said I'd never use it again."

The words hung in the air, as if they meant nothing. It was January and the fields were filled with snow. The fence lines had disappeared into drifts of white.

"Now you've really done it," she said.

Now I'd really done what couldn't be undone.

On the blacktop we passed Kriz's farm and my mother slowed automatically, and we both stared between the outbuildings to the wire enclosure where a peacock once lived, fanning its thousand-eyed tail. Snow filled the pen where the peacock strutted before the dowdy peahen female. How could such a magnificent tail evolve no matter how many eons; how could they, and we, exist in our Milky Way of fiery gases and cold space?

I watched the last of the dusking sun sink into the windbreaks, into the railroad crossing's signals. We drove past the farmhouse on the hill where we used to live and Mom slowed the Rambler. There was the pasture of hazel brush and the stock tank I tried to wish into a swimming pool, there were the apple trees–branches cocooned in ice and silvery blue with cold and moonlight, there stood the gate the donkey managed to escape from, the clothesline he used to scrape me off of his back. Human children our darling donkey, Jack, cared not a whit for, unless they were bearers of apples or corn; cats he liked for their winter warmth and he let them sleep on his back–two fur heating pads. He tolerated me, but ran if he saw a saddle, so I rode him bareback.

"I wish we'd stayed here. I wish I'd never married Al; what a mistake," Florence said. "Maybe you wouldn't have gone wild if we had." Renters lived there now and light glowed from the window that had been my bedroom. We took Old Jappa Road past Grandma's farm and the shagbark hickories. The white orchard. Here I rode my brother's bike in gravel to my piano lesson. Here I stopped to rest and licked the sweat from my arms to taste myself. Now the fields tried not to stare at me; they lowered their eyes.

The car heater seemed malicious. The burning in my left hand was only a month and a half old, yet I fanned myself as if it were 90 degrees. Three-fourths of my body shivered, one-fourth simmered in an unquenchable fire. The hand was already beginning its clench; the life that wasn't there burned. An afterimage, a red giant.

"Stephanie, I teach all day and can't take care of you. You're going to stay at Aunt Patsy's so Grandma can care for you."

"I can take care of myself."

"Baloney, you can't take care of yourself. If you could, why do I always have to clean up your messes and send you a bus ticket? Like that first time you were in North Carolina and were raped. Look at you! I don't call that taking care of yourself."

"I'd rather stay with you," I said.

"Oh, no, you're not staying with me. I can't trust you. You're going to Aunt Patsy's."

I was fallout. The shot that brought the slough pheasant down went on singing forever. I'd never be a child again. I'd never live like I did as a young girl; exploring the slough, visiting the drainage pipe that ran under the gravel road. Never crawl through, watch the rain, and after dark wait for eyes to appear, civet cats and raccoons.

That first night she warmed me her homemade tomato soup, what she always made the day after we stayed home from school sick. She didn't pebble mine with saltine crackers; instead, we sat together and I sucked the soup through my wired teeth.

"Stephanie, you were the healthiest of my three children," she said, more to herself than to me. "Well, was that boy worth it?"

⁂

I would never use my left arm again; the nerves that controlled its impulses had been shattered. The left side of my face would undergo two scar revisions but would always look slightly dented. A section of my jaw was replaced by metal and the bite of my teeth forever altered. The neurological pain, the nerves firing off into the netherland of my neck, would create *burning limb syndrome*, and there would be many medications and many therapies, and I would burn, bending my head to the pain as if bowing to it. I would take ten Advil a day. My mother never stopped hoping that some scientific breakthrough would get my arm working again. And although breakthroughs had indeed been made, they were too late for me–and for Florence.

Once, I grumbled and she lashed out, telling me that some mistakes were forever. That I'd brought it on myself. And she was right on both counts.

"Oh, Stephanie, until I broke my elbow, I never understood how it is for you. I had no idea. No idea. And you've never complained."

My dementia mother said that. And it was a watershed in our relationship. A reconciliation.

Bluebeard of the Sticks

On the third day of my mother's dying, my older brother, Joel, drives me through Cedar Rapids, and our childhood. The rusting Iowa Iron Works; the deserted Wilson's Meatpacking Plant, where the linemen silenced the terrified cows; and Little Bohemia, where the meatpackers, in their long black aprons, drank. We stop at Czech Town on 16th Avenue and buy kolaches from Sykora's, the family-owned bakery, which has for over a century sold rye breads and strudels and poppy seed rolls from the same glass counters in the same building, which just three years ago survived the great deluge, when the Cedar, the Wapsipinicon, and the Iowa Rivers overflowed their banks. The taste of the warm cherry filling reminds us both of our grandmother Emily, whose kolaches were the most sought-after at our country church potlucks.

We drive on. Cedar Rapids is not a beautiful Midwest metropolis. Its Quaker Oats and sorghum factories scent the air with fermenting grain. I fill my lungs with the sour smell, which comforts me. The Cedar River flows through the downtown's belly, branching on either side of City Island, which holds the jail. James Earl Ray, the assassin of Martin Luther King Jr., was imprisoned here for petty thievery in the 1960s. Later, Ray said it was the prettiest jail he had ever slept in, the river and the cedar trees growing along its banks. When breeze moves the leaves, it sounds like a second river; only this one, flowing in the air. I love this backwater city. I can desert it, but it never deserts me. Neither will the farm where I grew up, seven miles south of here, or the farm twenty miles due north, where we moved after Florence's marriage to Al.

"Al worked here," I tell my brother as we pass the empty yard of Wilson's Meatpacking, where the doomed cattle had been unloaded from the trucks.

Today, the closest slaughterhouse is an hour away, in Waterloo–a draw for hardworking immigrants. A sealed boxcar of illegal aliens from Mexico and Central America was recently discovered on a side track. Inside, all thirty men and boys were found dead, stiffened in blue contortions of asphyxiation. They'd been abandoned. Wherever there are slaughterhouses, filth, and entrails, there are undocumented laborers. The first slaughterhouse in Cedar Rapids gave jobs to immigrant Czechs after the American Civil War. Everything we call *Iowa,* including the very word, was taken from the indigenous Ioway peoples.

"I wasn't there for the craziness with Al," Joel says, hitting his blinker and guiding the car back onto 1st Avenue. "I'm glad that I was already in college. You and Brett bore the full brunt of it."

The traffic is so light that in no time we hit the outskirts of town. I'm expecting to see the Prairie Moon Ballroom, where Florence sometimes went on Wednesday nights for square dancing, and later, on Saturdays, for ballroom dancing. The blue neon no longer blinks its half-moon into the asphalt. The ballroom's gone, gutted by fire, the drafty behemoth melted into its foundation as if it were a giant marshmallow.

Joel drops me back at Village Ridge and I sit outside in the sun, mulling over *the crazy Al saga.* My mother deserved a good man; she was excellent wife material. To teach, to be educated, to be a mother, to serve God were all important to her, but to be a wife was her heart's desire. When reading the obituaries, she always noted the length of the deceased's marriage. "My goodness. She had sixty years of marriage. I had nine years. That's a spit." To my mother, a marriage's length was the yardstick of a successful life.

Florence had waited until she was 36 to marry. My father had been a man's man and, according to her, he hunted, fished, and rode a Harley-Davidson, yet he also studied religion, wrote poetry, and underlined proverbs. "Life is like a mirror. If you smile at it, it smiles back." What Florence had liked best about him was that he was *elevated.* My mother loved the quotes. When he sailed with the Merchant Marine and docked in exotic ports like Rio, he would stay onboard to watch the bloody-parrot sunsets and write poetry. Poetry, to her mind, was an exalted art. Years later, when I tried to practice the art, her opinion of it seemed to have slipped. In her estimation, the poetry written by the new generation was a degraded art, especially the unrhymed stuff. "Are you still writing that poetry that no one reads?" she would ask. The adventurous Florence, who rode from Iowa to Nevada on the back of her new husband's Harley, had been banished by worry and hard work.

After ten years of widowhood, ten years of teaching, of commuting from my grandmother's farm to Cedar Rapids, ten years of raising children alone, Florence began square dancing at the YWCA. She had joined Parents Without Partners. My brother Brett and I rejoiced. We wanted her to enjoy herself. We believed in the trickle-down effect. If Florence had more amusement, we would too. I think now of all that must have burdened her–the squelching of her Red Cross aspirations, the successful (still-living) men who had proposed marriage and whom she'd long ago rejected, her fatherless children, the anxiety that she called *nervousness.* "I am a nervous wreck," she'd often said. I thought of how, for my mother, the opportunity to laugh had waned.

The Prairie Moon Ballroom had been Florence's destination on that Saturday night in 1967. It would be her first date with Al. She had come from Hilda's Beauty Salon, her auburn hair a waterfall of shimmering ringlets.

"Stephy, do you want to use the bathwater before I empty it?" she called through the bathroom door. "No sense letting that expensive water drain away."

I entered the misty realm. I was sure Al had to be the most handsome man imaginable to make the farmhouse smell like nectarines and apricots. Earlier, she had poured a tablespoon of scented oil into her bath. But I tried not to look at my mother as she stepped into her underpants, and then her dress shields, squares of cotton backed by plastic that fit under the armpits by elastic loops. Dress shields were the bastard children of bloomers with back buttons, the detritus of a farm milieu where there were no dry cleaners or washing machines, only scrub boards and wringer washers that made laundry day Hell Day. A good dress of linen or silk or wool, or even cotton, had to be protected. I especially hated to see her stomach, a lovely loaf of rising bread snarled through with barbed-wire scars from her three Caesareans. The scar zigzagged and dimpled; it was red, then purple; it looked raw, as if it were still bleeding. A flesh zipper. How could any doctor have done that? How could I have done that, in my craven desire to be born? I wanted to kneel before her and ask forgiveness, but all I could think was *it'll never happen to me. If this is what a baby does to its mother, my body will never bear a child.*

She saw me looking. "They don't make the incisions so big and torn-up anymore. The new ones hardly show. It was that dumb doctor."

"Mom, you're going to a dance," I said. "Aren't you excited?"

Leaning over the sink, Florence smoothed on moisturizer. "Oh, phooey. At my age, you don't get excited."

I saw her as the mirror did. Her face was round, her lips full, her eyes blue. Loose powder flew from the powder puff over her cheeks. She was 54, but looked at least ten years younger.

"Who is this man you're going dancing with? Is he better than Harvey?" I asked. My mother, who spent almost none of the money she earned on herself, who gave herself so little pleasure, had a date. I'd seen her dress up twice before tonight, for dancing with the old bachelor Harvey. She was a widow who loved to dance.

"His name is Al," Florence had said, applying makeup and digging in her almost-used-up *Real Red* lipstick with a bobby pin. "I think he has only high school. He's a foreman at Wilson's Meatpacking Plant. Give me something to blot my lips." I handed her a Kleenex. "Don't waste a good Kleenex; give me toilet paper." She blotted her lips with the square of toilet paper.

I heard a car pull in. "Mom, he's here!"

"Help me with my dress."

I held the black dress as she stepped into its skirt, which was filled out by a black can-can petticoat, its back sheer, with see-through sleeves. Amazingly, the dress shields didn't show anywhere. If I hadn't known better, I might have thought she was purposely trying to dress provocatively. She sprayed Blue Grass behind each ear and on her wrists. My brother Brett went to open the farmhouse door. My oldest brother was missing his chance to meet Al. Joel had graduated at 16, and was already studying physics in college.

Soon, Al was sitting on the couch. His blue eyes were watery, although he didn't stare at the carpet like the bachelor from Shueyville had. But he didn't look directly at us either. Mom had gone to two dances with Harvey, but wasn't interested in him because he lived with his mother. "I could never marry him," Florence had said. "He's a mama's boy. What would we talk about all day?" I'd agreed. We could never marry Harvey. Not that skinny man in a blue suit, the trousers too short for his legs when he sat on the loveseat and crossed them. Harvey's thinning hair was the same color as the stain on the chair arms. He wore bifocals, and his bony fingers tapped his knee as though they were kindling while he waited to help Mom on with her coat.

Al was broad-shouldered, over six feet tall, more man, younger; in fact, seventeen years younger than Florence. He chose the couch, not the loveseat, in order get a wider view. His eyes took in the living room the way they'd already surveyed the land between our farm and my grandmother's farm down the road, as if they were counting the acres. *Black soil, richest in the world.* Now he sat in the best room in the farmhouse, although calling it a living room was a misnomer since no one set foot in it on weekends, except me, in order to clean. On weekdays, after the school bus dropped us off and before Florence arrived home from teaching, Brett and I used it for wrestling and fighting and laughing. I might hide in the stairwell, jump out, spit at him, and then run. He would give chase, tackle me, sit on my stomach, and spit in my face. After that, throw rugs might be grabbed and swung, ambushes carried out with a broom or squirt gun; we, all the while, laughing madly. Then hurriedly straighten the living room before Mom drove up in the blue Rambler.

The living room, newly redecorated with thick beige carpet and a mirrored buffet, its velvet loveseats and rockers, and moldering antiques before Florence refinished, now looked expensive. I watched Al's eyes sink into the burgundy loveseat. His eyes lit (crawled) along the tin bookshelves, and I felt certain our suitor had never been in a house that had a bookshelf, though I could have told him the bookshelves were tin, cost ten dollars, and had come on the mail truck with the seven-dollar set of encyclopedias, whose entries were no bigger than the ingredients on the back of a Jiffy corn muffin box.

Giggling, I sat on the couch and listened to him talk, although he said very little. His reddish hair was clipped short, his nose flat, the nostrils distended. His knuckles were red and threaded with wiry amber hair. Yet, if you stood far enough back, he could pass for Cedar Rapids handsome. Brett and I hardly knew how to act with a grown man in the house. The next afternoon, I would hear Florence on the phone, telling Aunt Patsy that he *carried a suit well.*

I approved of the practiced way Al helped Florence into her red coat with the slippery silk lining. But before leaving on her date, my mother checked each electrical appliance, unplugging the toaster, the can opener, the desk lamp, the family-room humidifier; worried that a fire might start while she was away. No matter that her two teenagers would be at home.

After they drove away, I took my bath. The coils of the space heater glowed. I undressed and got into the tub's silky water. It was cold. I closed my eyes, imagining that I was floating in sun-nuzzled apricots. But the apricot orchard didn't last and the water turned to ice. I got out, wrapped in a towel, and quickly pulled on my sweatshirt and pants. *Al* was a plain name, I thought; a common one that you might pick if you couldn't think of anything else. Not like *Philip Osborne.* Not like *Joel James* or *Brett John* or *Stephanie Emily.*

That night, I waited up for Mom. I could hear the car from a long way off, the gravel crackling under its tires, growing louder and louder. The car pulled in. Murmurs at the door.

"Did you have fun?" I asked, the moment after Mom hung up her coat. Florence looked refreshed, which she rarely did after a day of teaching school. Even her curls bounced.

"Oh, it was fine," she said with a smile. "The band played my kind of music. Not that jumping-around stuff. We danced almost every dance."

"So, do you like him?" Her lipstick had worn off, and I wondered if Al had kissed her.

"He's a good dancer," she said, before sending me to bed.

That's how the Bluebeard of the Sticks entered my life. On his twinkle toes.

The next time Al visited, he sat on the loveseat, while Florence, again fresh from Hilda's Beauty Salon, shook out her tinted curls and put on another gauzy black dress that had come from some secret compartment in her closet. I'd never seen it before–and I had explored every nook and cranny in the farmhouse. On the third date, Florence wore a new necklace, and around her wrist, a matching bracelet–gifts from Al.

By their fourth date, Brett and I noticed that Al's nose ran habitually, and a drop of water sometimes hung from one of his nostrils. He tried to sniff the drop, which resembled a pearl onion, back up into his nose. But the drop refused to stay in his nose and soon dripped out. Brett wondered how long Al Baugh would last. They danced at Armar and Dance-Mor on Saturdays, then Wednesdays at the Prairie Moon Ballroom. In the half-glitter, where blowing tinsel and a blue light gave the dance floor glamour, Al courted Florence.

Two months passed.

"What do you kids think?" she asked, showing us her ring. Al had given my mother a diamond, a huge rock on a white-gold platinum band.

I thought of that bit of snot dripping from his nose. "It's beautiful, Mom," I said.

"I've decided to marry him. He's got a farm just outside Central City. We're going to live in the old house that's there until he builds the new one."

I clapped my hands, happy for all of us. I liked Al–runny nose and all.

"It's a second marriage for both of us."

My ears perked up. "What happened to his first wife?"

Florence eyed my fingers. It was mealtime and I hadn't

washed my hands. "He said his wife had Fuller Brush salesmen."

"I bet," I said. "That sounds like a big, fat lie." Even then, Fuller Brush salesmen were almost extinct. They were late-night TV jokes. Only, we didn't have TV, except at Grandma's.

"They were married fifteen years and had four kids, but Al claims the last two aren't his."

I chuckled. "What did she look like?"

"I only met his ex-wife once. Her hair was up in rollers. She was sitting in a messy house, drinking pop and watching television."

* *

The wedding. I sat in the front row of the First Presbyterian Church, near Ely, Iowa. It was the same country church where Florence had married my father. This time, no white gown, no Stephanotis, no Baby's Breath. My mother wore a beige knit suit, and Al, his blue square-dancing suit. My uncle Fred traveled from Illinois to perform the ceremony.

Florence and Al honeymooned in Hot Springs, Arkansas. The railroad used to bring thousands of fun-seekers to the "Las Vegas of the Ozarks." Ten million gallons of water a day gurgled through the bathhouses. Florence sent brochures and postcards of the Ozarks' magic. Dense forests. Flowering dogwood. Blue ash. Swamp chestnut. Mountains and natural springs. Hot Springs, where 19th Century women in white dresses had balanced themselves on logs over the boiling mud. In a dog-trot cabin, the original Majestic Hotel, the women had changed into black frocks and lowered themselves into the mud. When they emerged, every pore had been scoured and cleansed. It was at the Majestic Hotel where Florence and Al consummated their marriage. There, Al said to my mother, "You have the body of a 15-year-old." I will always like him for telling her that.

It was July, their honeymoon week. I was 13, on the cusp of 14. My pastor uncle stayed for a week's visit with my grandmother, who lived one field away from our farm on the hill. It was ours in name only, as it also belonged to our grandmother Emily. Nights, my brother and I slept at Grandma's; days, we were allowed free rein on the hill farm. On the third day of my mother's honeymoon, I lied to my grandmother, telling her I'd be practicing my recital piece, "Born Free," on the piano all afternoon at the house on the hill, and that she could expect me for supper. Instead, I rode my bike to my friend Sandy Lint's trailer a mile away to see a boy I liked, who, along with Sandy's boyfriend, was spending the afternoon there. Thrill of the forbidden, the first time I'd ever ridden off on my own, not telling a soul where I was going. I was boy-crazy, but it wasn't really about the boy. It was about me, desperate to be something special to someone. We had just settled into a game of kiss-tag, when my pastor uncle's red car pulled up. He strode up the wrinkle of a driveway and, without saying a word to Sandy, lifted my bike, carried it to the car, and stowed it in the trunk. I slunk down in the passenger's seat; having always looked up to my uncle, he was now looking down on me. "Stephy, you're a bad girl." I was shamed for the rest of my mother's honeymoon. These were the first signs of my reckless inferiority fueling a lie-face sneakiness.

Hunger Wafers

We married Al and moved from our hill farm to his before the new school year began. My mother packed the last of our dishware, wrapping each plate and mug in newspaper, while Brett and I traveled with Al in his pickup, transporting our household furniture and belongings load by load. His farmstead lay outside Central City, a town with a population of 1,000, twenty-five miles to the north. I had always lived with my grandmother, or a minute away from her by car, two minutes by bicycle, ten minutes on foot, or fifteen minutes on Jack the donkey's cantankerous back.

I wanted to take Grandma with us. I wanted to take Jack, too, but Florence said no. Al had no desire for a bad-tempered, hee-hawing donkey, and Jack was to be gifted to Joel's former biology teacher as a pet for his children (not a laboratory experiment). Florence loved Jack, and yet, she had given him up. Our grandmother wanted to stay where she was. She would keep our black-and-white mongrel, Cindy. How these animals of our past resonate. They call to us with their unknown fates. *How could you have left us behind?* Later I'll learn that they're not left behind at all, but following us for the rest of our days.

We drove down the gravel roads and the little speckled hills I'd always known. I rode in the cab with Al, while Brett bounced in back with the furniture. When Al reached into his bib overall pocket for a can of Copenhagen snuff, my mouth popped open. The tobacco shreds crawled between his pinched yellowed fingers like wet, dark worms. A little pellet formed in his cheek. I smelled the raw, sharp tang of snuff. I'd never seen anyone dip snuff before. It was something only toothless hillbillies did.

The blue pickup jerked. Al had to keep stick-shifting into third gear and fourth. "You're going to work," he said, his tongue moving the ball of snuff from one cheek to the other, then under his front lip, his front teeth slightly overlapping. He pulled up to a stop sign and unrolled the window, letting loose a grasshopper stream of tobacco juice. "You and your brother have been sitting on your duffs all along, letting your mother do everything." He spat another stream out. "That's about to come to an end!" He wiped his hand along his cornmeal-colored T-shirt and bib overalls.

I had always thought we were poor. Now I saw that, despite the awful clothes we wore, my brother and I had been raised in relative prosperity. Al had come from poor.

I gazed into the side mirror and noticed Brett rising and falling in the bed of the pickup, being jostled along with the buffet and oak kitchen table.

Al drove on. The drop of snot water was leaking down his nostril, jiggling with the cracks in the highway. Suddenly, I didn't want to be near him; not in the truck, not in a house, not in the same state. I didn't want us to be married to him anymore. At the next turnoff, he stopped and reached under the seat for a long-necked bottle. The bottle was unlike any bottle I'd ever seen; its label pictured a hunter carrying three dead pheasants. *Three Feathers Whiskey.* My first sight of bourbon didn't feel thrillingly exotic. I knew it wasn't the Riviera inside. No frosted triangle glasses, speared olives, or shaved ice. Like what was served in *Film Town* movie magazines. No liquor the color of rubies. Distilled in this bottle, along with the alcohol, must be the pheasants killed in an autumn slough. Did Florence know that Al drank? Mom–who had never taken a drink in her life.

He chuckled. "Watch the load on the west end. Your brother doesn't know which end of a cow is up."

The wood legs of the kitchen chairs were covered with beads of dust and stuck up like tipped cows. The reedy ditches wore their festive dust. "How am I doing on that end?" he asked. I peered into the side mirror. I saw only my own round face, with large, brown, bovine eyes.

Al swigged from his Three Feathers before the bottle vanished under the seat as quickly as it had appeared. We were on Highway 12, heading toward Central City. A mile before the city limits, we took a turn. Nearing the property, the ditches stopped thriving. The roadsides, crowded with wild oats and cattails, began to flatten and thin. Stray strands of brittle prairie grass. There, atop a knoll, his farm welcomed us. On the mailbox, ALLEN BAUGH was printed. Run-down, tarpaper-shingled, the house was gray like a sink of potato peelings. An empty feeder trough. Next to a freshly painted barn and chicken coop, the gray house lorded over the bare yard. A picture window looked out from the house's north side, where a PIONEER FEEDS sign had been nailed next to a weather vane.

We had arrived at the Castle of Bluebeard.

Al's blue eyes twinkled as he unscrewed the screen door to make room for our furniture. None of the good things, especially the burgundy velvet loveseat and rocker, had made the trip. The better things wouldn't be brought here until Al built the promised new house. I shuffled inside. Mice pellets shuddered out of the cupboards and a sheen of coal dust from the cellar lay over everything. Although it was August, you could feel the raw cold that the old, groaning house held.

"Looks like you two can start right to work," he said. "The floor needs sweeping."

I smarted off. "I don't see a broom."

He snorted and unlatched the hook-and-eye door that led to the cellar. A puff of coal dust belched out when he reached in. "I can help you out there."

Still in its wrapper, the broom had to have been the only new thing in the house. I swept, while Al watched me. The walls appeared defeated. The light fixtures dangled like fizzled hopes.

Al's sawdust eyebrows rose. "Not just in the middle of the floor, young lady. Get that broom into the corners," he commanded, pointing to piles of what might have been moldy seed corn. "And you and your brother will feed the sow I've just bought. Her name is Bonnie, and she's in the barn."

I sighed. So this was where our hasty marriage had landed us. But he was stuck with us too–an almost 14-year-old girl and a just-turned-16-year-old boy, useless eaters. If two teenagers were part of the package, Al likely thought Florence should pay for our groceries, not him. He believed my mother was rich, but he would soon learn that he was dead wrong. Everything belonged to my grandmother; the two farms and the land. No matter. Useless eaters would work under his command. Al was the lead cow of the household, and we were his followers.

Florence would later explain, "He's lower class than we are. And he's conscious of it. And his mother is funny. She always wanted money from him, and he resented it. I think she drank."

Al had big dreams of tending hogs, of breeding sows, and raising piglets.

I was crazy to get off the farm, to fall in love with town motorcycles and black fishnet stockings. All of my stories of this period begin *when we married Al.* I embellish for the black comedy of it all. But what did my mother feel? What had she felt in Hot Springs on her honeymoon, when she had been riding with her new husband and said that he should turn left, and he had slammed on the brakes, flushed red in the face, and barked at her to never tell him what to do. Ever.

These days, the cold is not cold like it was that winter of my mother's marriage to Al. We were going hungry. When the gray snowdrifts had hardened against the house, and nothing remained of the Nabisco Nilla Wafers but crumbs, and the last can of wax beans had been eaten, Florence would drive us to Vinton to spend the weekend with Aunt Patsy and Uncle Douglas. Once again, the younger sister sought shelter with the luckier one. Aunt Patsy was four years older than Florence and had married a fellow teacher. After the war, Uncle Douglas had gone to dental school on the G.I. Bill.

"Steffer, how are you?" Aunt Patsy asked, holding the door open. My brother and I were fine and safe now that we'd arrived here. I see now from a distance how humiliating this must have been for my mother. Once again, she is *the girl behind the door*, watching her older brother and sister and their friends sing around the piano. Only, now the girl has a line of disappointment etched on either side of her mouth. Florence had been self-conscious and shy.

I took off my coat, glad for the warmth everywhere, not just over one grate like in the shivering downstairs of Al's farmhouse. The house smelled of citrus, and the sheer lavender curtains billowed with balmy breath from the heating vents. The kitchen countertops were a confetti-patterned enamel, and spotless, except for a box of jelly-filled donuts and cinnamon twists and cream puffs. A stainless steel sink's faucet gushed fluoride water. Lukewarm and softened, to my 14-year-old mouth, town water tasted better than the iciness of farm well-water. My brother and I sat at the cushioned kitchen table, which was shaped like a café booth. From here we could admire, and not let out of our sight, the wondrous refrigerator, with its white shelving and bunches of rinsed red grapes, its slices of lunch meat salami and cheese, olives and pickles. In its freezer, the Eskimo Bars and Fudgsicles, the gallons of Neapolitan and vanilla ice cream lay dreaming–a magical, always-replenished refrigerator. An ice maker whirred cubes to chill the bottles of Fresca and Diet Rite. These were beautiful foods. Aunt Patsy let us serve ourselves, to graze and eat whatever and however much we wanted.

Soon my aunt shooed us into the living room. She and Florence wanted to talk. "You children take your plates and go watch TV."

I sat on the dark green sectional couch next to my uncle's recliner and his pipe rack and ashtray. I leafed through his magazine holder, where *Field & Stream* shared space with my aunt's *Photoplays*. A cut-glass mirror covered an entire wall, surrounded by built-in bookcases and porcelain tea cups and saucers; my uncle's medical tomes peered out, with their arcane hieroglyphics, between the gold-gilt encyclopedias.

I listened to my aunt's and mother's voices filtering from the kitchen. They spoke in Czech and mixed-in English words, then vice versa, the languages twining together like strands of dough. We were the poor relations, my oldest brother Joel in college, his tuition paid for by my uncle.

"Honestly, Florence." Aunt Patsy clucked her tongue. "Brett and Steffer dress like ragamuffins."

"That's the least of my worries," Florence said. "Al's stopped buying groceries. He's giving me only ten dollars a week."

"A man who won't buy groceries? Who ever heard of such a thing?" My aunt kept her voice low. Florence had always mentioned that Aunt Patsy was an alto, while she was a soprano. Our father had fallen in love with her beautiful singing voice. She hinted that a soprano was preferable to an alto; that, at least in music, Florence had been the lucky one.

The TV consumed my brother's attention. Saturday afternoon wrestlers recoiled across the ring as if the ropes were slingshots. They body-slammed each other onto the mats and jumped on each other's chests. The thuds and groans excited the crowd. The Viking, with his horned helmet and fur cape, roared as he swaggered into the ring. Captain Kidd, wearing an eye patch, waved a cutlass. His red face and whiskey-colored hair reminded me of Al. Those same sawdust eyebrows, each splinter a balloon popper. Brett stretched out on the carpet. Warm. Everything soothing here. I was fascinated by my uncle's pipes, the canister of cherry tobacco. I touched the bite marks of his teeth on the pipe stem. I chose a pipe and, pretending to smoke it, set my teeth where my uncle's had clenched, and I inhaled. My saliva against his. I tasted the tobacco. The stickiness of nicotine. I discovered I liked the taste of the forbidden in my mouth.

The voices in the kitchen rose and fell.

"Al wants the trust funds. The five thousand dollars Phil's folks left for each of their grandchildren."

"You shouldn't have told him about that," Aunt Patsy said. Again, her tongue clucked.

Florence's voice sharpened. "I know, Patsy. I'm so dumb sometimes."

"It's not yours to give." I could picture Aunt Patsy shaking her head.

Then an undercurrent of Czech. Mysterious, guttural mutter. I heard mention of the diamond engagement ring. A huge diamond on a platinum band. Simple, but stunning.

"He took your diamond engagement ring back?"

"Yes, Patsy. He twisted it off my finger."

Now I pictured a line forming between Aunt Patsy's brows. "Honestly, Florence, what an awful man. He marries you, then treats you like dirt."

The taste in my mouth soured. Not even a Fudgsicle could sweeten it.

"Where is he tonight?" Aunt Patsy asked.

"Probably in Little Bohemia or drinking in the barn. He keeps whiskey there."

I wondered if he wasn't putting on his suit and going to Dance-Mor to pick up widows.

"He shouldn't have twisted it off your finger," Aunt Patsy repeated. "Honestly." She was opening the refrigerator, reaching for her red grapes. Her favorites. Chilled.

"All right, Patsy, you said it once. But what should I do?" Florence asked. "What does Douglas think?"

Douglas was finishing his Saturday half day of work. Behind the accordion door there was another living room, an even prettier one, with a fireplace and gold-threaded furniture. The inner sanctum where my aunt and uncle entertained their bridge-and-party set. Another accordion door led to the dental office that paid for all this–one cavity and filling at a time. I liked to sit in the dental chair when the patients were gone, when the waiting room and its red Charms-sucker couches had emptied. I loved the smell of dentistry; the hiss of the drill and Waterpik, the scent of the modeling clay in which impressions for dentures were taken. The citrus odor stronger here and mixed with cinnamon mouthwash and hand soap. The FM radio off, but Nat Cole's "Unforgettable" lingering in the air.

The accordion door whooshed open and Uncle Douglas scurried into the kitchen. He was whistling. Even in those pre-AIDS days, my uncle constantly washed his hands. He did not wear gloves. Black, wavy hair, glasses, white dental jacket, his whistling completed the package. Brett paid no attention to the fact that our future was being discussed in the kitchen. He was transfixed by the meaty wrestlers, their ham-hock arms lifted over their opponents' heads like Stone Age clubs, beckoning the frenzied shouts of the crowd, who wanted to see the refs vanish and the bloodletting begin.

Uncle Douglas joined the kitchen debate. He did not speak Czech and now all the talking was in English. I stared at the fireplace's mantel and the blown-glass vases with crystal stoppers. Forest green and lilac. Like orchids.

I was riveted. What would they advise Florence to do? I desperately longed to run wild. A faucet went on.

"Florence, have you considered divorce?" Uncle Douglas asked, matter-of-factly.

"I don't know, Douglas," she replied.

I heard the words. *Annulment. Separation.* I flipped through a *Photoplay* movie magazine and skimmed over the doings of the celebrities. *Sinatra marries Mia Farrow.* An elopement. Her fawn eyes and boy's haircut above a terrain of flickering candles and long-stemmed dinner goblets. *Liz leaves Eddie Fisher for Richard Burton.* Divorce.

I decided I would never marry.

⁂

I still do not know Florence's real feelings for her second husband, but when she was married to Al, her vigilance over her children slackened. Having a man made her happy. Even a cheapskate like Al. No longer did she rise to make oatmeal breakfasts as she used to. No longer did we have Bible readings before bedtime. No longer did Florence insist on us practicing the piano each day.

It was during this marriage that I myself fell in love. A junior, age 16, and able to drive, Ronnie Simmen would come to pick me up for school in his father's white Oldsmobile. He would drive by once and honk, waking Al and my mother in their bedroom, which faced the gravel road. That was my cue to run down the lane and wait by the mailbox while he backed the Oldsmobile into the cattle turnaround. On his second pass, I was ready. Freshly bathed, wearing fishnets, my rabbit fur jacket, and white lipstick. Just a 16-year-old boy picking up a 14-year-old girl and driving her to school. But we didn't go directly to school. I slid in across the front seat (neither of us wearing seat belts), my leg settling next to his. I was a black rose. A wooden booth at Danceland, ready to be gouged with initials and hearts.

"Hello, Morocco Mole," he said, pressing on the gas.

And we were off, free of the dreary battleship farmhouse and the empty refrigerator. Ronnie smelled good, his clothes crisp. I teased him about his mother starching his jeans.

"Does she iron your sheets too?" I asked.

He offered me Wrigley's Spearmint gum, and I took it. KCRG played on the radio; the darker drum solo of Iron Butterfly's "In-A-Gadda-Da-Vida" swept away the prettified harmonies of the Bee Gees. Ronnie drove us deeper into the country, where we parked in the bright sun. Through the windshield, the broken cornstalks left in the winter fields watched us kissing; a few husks waved from the barbed-wire fence. I was willful, and determined to throw myself away.

I liked Ronnie's smell of brown paper sacks from Sauer's Jack-N-Jill, where he bagged groceries. Like the old days on the hill farm when my mother would stop at the Me Too Grocery after her teaching day ended. The scent of her return home had been brown paper sack and celery. Now that we had so little to eat, someone who smelled of celery was someone to love. I mooned over Ronnie. After school, he went to his sacker's job, and I took the bus home. I waited for the next morning to touch his hands. He had scraped his fingernails with the box cutter at the Jack-N-Jill, and there were lumpy peaks and valleys on his nails. I relished touching them, as if, to be lovely, a thing needed to be mutilated. My aunt had given me a Tabu cologne stick for Christmas, and I mistakenly thought it was a roll-on deodorant. I knew that I was in love with Ronnie because my underarms sweated so much.

Later, he went on to bomb Laos.

⁂

That year, I did not see autumn or spring; I only saw winter, like I'd never seen it before. Winters in a farmhouse were different from winters elsewhere. The drafts through the unchinked lathe and plaster walls whistled in, the screen doors rattled. A farmhouse usually has two doors: a screen door for the summer breeze and a solid wood door with its pane of glass. On farms, the screen doors and screen windows would be taken off in the fall and the storm windows put on. Double panes of glass kept out the wind. On Al's farm, the screens had been left on and one pane of glass kept the cold out, and there were no registers in my room. I slept under my grandmother's feather tick, in my own winter. I dreamed blizzards and snow hills. I huddled under the field of dead goose feathers. In my snow hill, I waited for rescue by my upperclassman boyfriend.

⁂

A lifetime later, after I had turned 40 and Florence 81, she drove me by Al's farm in the car left her by her third husband, Gordon. We turned off Highway 12, onto the gravel road. On top of the hill, a purple silo loomed. "It's a sharp curve. I'm only doing this for you. Ugh, that ugly dust. Roll your window up," Florence said, reaching in her purse for another scarf.

Now home from New York City, decades gone from this place, I felt like I was 14 again. We neared the pig farmer's property, and the ditches once more stopped thriving. The roadsides, which had been crowded with oats, timothy, and cattails, again began to thin.

At the top of the hill, two houses stood six feet apart. No front lawn. A modern ranch house, painted turquoise, situated next to the familiar two-story gray farmhouse with tarpaper shingles.

"Go slow," I said, pointing. "See that upstairs window? That was my room!" I had unsnapped my seat belt.

"Don't think you're getting out," my mother said.

"I know that, Mom."

Florence flipped her clip-on sunglasses up. "Would you look? He finally built that house he promised me. They say he took all of his fourth wife's money. She's suing him. I hope she wins. Just so he doesn't see us."

There it was. The battleship house with the coal furnace in the cellar; the unheated upstairs where Brett and I had slept, our breath rising in a white mist above the feather tick. There was the barn, still better-looking than the farmhouse; the lane I pictured knotted with ice and cut by hooves, where I had carried buckets of lardy shanks, butchered piglets still warm from the sow. The window where the tinsel Christmas tree had stood, Tammy Wynette and George Jones twanging *Deck the Halls* from Al's hi-fi. Behind that tiny window, stuffed with a gunny sack, was the bathroom, where I had poured hydrogen peroxide over my hair, turning it bird-shit orange; the claw-and-ball tub I bathed in before dawn; the dash, wrapped in a towel, up the frigid stairs.

Al had been good at courting women. Taking them to Danceland, his hand at the small of their backs, he had known how to guide a lady onto the dance floor. *He carried a suit well.* After the marriage, I rarely saw the suit. He did not go to church with us, and no longer side-stepped Florence over the dance floor, except for a single occasion at New Year's when out came the blue suit and Old Spice. Aunt Patsy had found a picture of him in the *Cedar Rapids Gazette*. Mr. Allen Baugh, of rural Central City, in a square-dance circle at the Czech Museum, holding the hand of a "girl"–looking, in late middle age, even healthier than he had in decades past. "He's available," my aunt had giggled. Divorced for the fourth time, the Bluebeard of the Sticks was once again on the prowl.

That day when I was home from New York City and Florence and I had driven past Al's farm, she seemed free of either love or hate for him. He was part of a too-distant past.

"What did you see in him?" I had questioned. "We ate piglets that died of hog cholera. He tried to starve us. When his piglets died, he bawled." I remembered lying in the frigid upstairs, hearing that grown man sob and make squeaking sounds. My brother and I had laughed. We could not stop.

"For your information, Miss Smarty Pants, there was nobody else interested in a widow with three children. He was a good dancer, and he was the only one who asked."

"We ate those sick piglets for a year."

"I would never have eaten dirty meat. You know how I am about germs."

"Piglet and three-bean salad," I said, envisioning my plate, the piglet pink and wrinkled like a baby's foot swimming in brown grease. The piglet had been a baby too, one that had never lived. Stillbirths. Victims of the hog cholera that had killed in a hard winter.

"You just be quiet," my mother said, the way she did when she drove, complaining of having a one-track mind and needing to concentrate on the highway. "Veal. That's what they call it in fancy restaurants. Young pork loin. Wasn't that good enough for you?"

"Veal is beef, not pork."

"Don't you think I know? My father butchered our own meat. Pig and cow!"

She wore a frozen expression on her face, like the winter night that Al's sow had delivered stillbirths. The hog cholera Al had somehow let creep in, the piglets dying just as they were born. Florence had that expression as she hoisted the pieces of a butchered piglet into the kitchen sink. "Al said we could still eat them," she had said. I carried in buckets, tracking the linoleum with dirty, pinkish ice, the meat whorled with tallow that reminded me of Shirley Temple curls. When Florence turned on the cold water, I ran outside.

Now I think of that cold barn and the sow wanting to be delivered of her litter; how all of them died, and soon her life would be finished too. I think of the agony of living creatures.

Florence and I drove back to Village Place. It was dinnertime for those residents who purchased meal plans, which my mother didn't. Four to a table, many were well-dressed couples, and we would have to walk through the lobby, close to the dining room. "Stephanie, if you ever do anything for me in your life, you will wipe that black stuff off your eyes before we go in. Pull your shirt down. Your belly button shows. I'm sick of looking at it. Nobody wants to see your belly button. You're not a teenager anymore."

"I know that, Mom," I said, yanking down my shirt. But there was no way I could wipe the black stuff from my eyes.

Townies

I think now of the pig farmer's kitchen and the eighteen months Florence was married to him. The refrigerator with nothing much in it and the table with four cracked plates. Three-bean salad in its onion-and-vinegar brine. Kidney. Lima. Wax. And, in the oven, the baking piglet loins crisped with fat. Al coming into the kitchen just shaved. I can see nicks on his chin. (In the bathroom I examine his electric razor, the thorn-like whiskers a mix of reddish and cornmeal-colored stubble.) I hear him walking in his stockinged feet from the downstairs bedroom–the only hot room in the coal-heated farmhouse. A clothesline rope that a blanket hangs from divides the newlyweds' quarters from the living room. He is taking his place at the head of the table. Picking up his fork, his eyes are alert, suspicious. Glancing out into the field of forlorn cornstalks left behind by the harvester, no one at the table is imagining happiness. A lifetime later, I feel a strange empathy for him, sitting at the table, his wife's teenage children watching him. We wait for the drop of nasal water to leak from a nostril, listening for him to snort, to make the whinnying sound. Brett and I kick and nudge each other under the table, about to erupt into laughter; that wild hilarity that only the young can feel in their fresh, undamaged bodies. It was no terrible trial for my brother and me to live on Al's beaten-down farm. We might have gladly suffered it if Al had tried to make our mother happy. And, later, Al told the neighbors that Florence made him sit on the floor so her children could have chairs. Al never sat on the floor, but he must have felt as if he had.

What were my mother's feelings for Al when she was middle-aged, not old? The woman who would in some distant day say to me during an argument, "I'm human. I'm human too." Did the human she was want the marriage to succeed?

I only know that after he began drinking in the barn and not buying groceries, Florence had to go back to substitute teaching. On one occasion, she taught at Central City High, the school that Brett and I attended. She was *Mrs. Baugh.*

The high school's wooden floors had buckled. The lockers were battered and crisscrossed with kick marks, and even the concrete steps at the entrance sagged. Fire escapes clung to the brick building like mangled grasshoppers in a drought-blackened cornfield. The school held a little over 200, half of them farm kids and half of them town kids. In Central City, *townies* didn't look down on the *hayseeds*, because everyone was hick. The FFA (Future Farmers of America) guys hung out together and the townie upperclassmen rode motorcycles and called themselves *Da Club.* They roared up and down the tree-lined streets of a tiny town that drowsed on either side of the Wapsipinicon River. It was that town that I had my eye on.

And there were the tough rural kids, raised in poverty, like he Lathrops and the Silvers. Poor families with five troublemaking boys each, the elder brothers blazing the path to dropout failure. Their reputations preceded them. They gave the teachers hell, and then quit school on their 16th birthdays. The Lathrop boys were likely bored with their six-packs of Schlitz as they waited for the drug tsunami about to flood Iowa. One day in the distant future, the eldest Lathrop would die of a heart attack in the passenger's seat of a car driven by his younger brother. They were in Missouri on a bender. The younger brother, not known for being bright, would drive his brother all the way back to Mercy Hospital in Cedar Rapids, drive hundreds of miles with a corpse for a passenger. The days had not turned that dark yet. Beer was still the drug of choice; cases of it purchased at Bob's Tavern by a 21-year-old brother for the others, who packed themselves into a car and cruised the countryside boozing and then vomiting in ditches.

The day Florence substitute-taught civics, the Silvers and Lathrops were both represented in her class. Larry Silver, the good-looking football player with greasy brown hair that swirled up from the crown of his forehead, blew spit wads through the empty cartridge of a Bic pen into the back row, where the sleepers rested their foreheads on the weighty Constitution. Few scholars in the class. As the wads of spit-flecked paper flew, Florence told Larry to give her the Bic pen. "You're not telling me what to do," he likely said, his lip curling. I wasn't there. My mother, who knew her grammar, who could teach anything, including math and Latin, rattled easily. She was not a disciplinarian.

She would have washed her hose out in a bucket and hung them to dry in the bathroom the night before. She wore garters and there was likely a small run in her stockings, or maybe more than one. Nylons had been too precious during WWII, when petroleum products had fed the fighting machine, and hosiery was a petro by-product. You did not throw them away. Her laddered stockings might have been acceptable in front of adults, but not teenagers. Teen eyes studied every freckle and dimple, every nook and cranny of Florence's brown pencil skirt, shiny from the iron, her green sweater brightened by clip-on earrings and a string of costume beads. Here was a newly married woman whose husband refused to buy groceries because he had discovered her children had a trust of $5,000 each, left them by their paternal grandparents. He wanted the $15,000. Because of that, Florence stood before the class as a substitute teacher. Her costume pin, a snowflake of cut glass, flashed its two-dollar beauty. She had deciphered the lesson plan. The class would discuss Article III of the Constitution. She read, "The judicial Power of the United States shall be vested in one supreme Court, and in such inferior Courts as the Congress may from time…." She had not finished the sentence before there was an uproar. Judgment. Giggling. She turned to face the blackboard. They judged the backs of Florence's legs, crisscrossed with varicose veins that came from having children.

The hour must have stretched out endlessly. The class engaged in substitute-teacher antics. Elastic cords between desks to trip her, raucous laughter. Larry Silver, the ringleader of the humiliate-and-attack brigade.

"Be quiet," she probably said, searching to find his name on the seating chart. But no one was sitting in their assigned seat.

"Go to hell, Granny Goodwitch," he mouthed off.

It could have been something cruel like that. And her farm-girl hand rose up and she slapped him. The girl behind the door in chore clothes rose up and slapped Larry's mouth. Today, that slap would have ended Florence's teaching career. The school would have been sued, my mother vilified. But, then, Larry charged out of the room and into the principal's office and quit school. He would be missed on the football team, although the Central City Wildcats always lost.

That day, I rode the bus home and heard Denise, a pretty junior with eyes like blue soft-boiled eggs, talk about civics class and the weird teacher, Mrs. Baugh, who had slapped Larry Silver. My face burned, ashamed of my mother, yet angry at Denise for calling her *weird.* I sighed with relief, grateful that my last name was *Dickinson.*

⁂

We had moved out of Al's farmhouse and Florence rented an apartment in Central City. My mother and I shared the one bedroom and Brett slept on the couch. It was here that I noticed my brother becoming handsome. The girls thought so, too. They took note of his dark brown eyes and hair, his cleft chin. No longer the burr haircut of early farm days, no longer chubby, my father's compact physique, combined with my grandmother's kindness, fit well on him. I wondered where his gentle nature came from. Such goodness.

When we lived on our grandmother's farm and Florence would announce that after church we were going to Cedar Rapids to eat, I'd clap my hands. We could either dine in the Rambler at Henry's Hamburgers, where a burger was 15 cents, or we could go to Bishop's Cafeteria, with its buffet of scrumptious salads and desserts. Chilled custards with sweet brown skins, chocolate graham cracker pie under chocolate shavings and curls of whipped cream. Pineapple rings and cherries adorning slabs of country ham, iced tea relaxing in tall glasses with lemons and straws. All loveliness and fun; even the red bathroom in the basement was delicious. "It's up to you kids," Florence would say. A buffet cost much more than a hamburger. Brett had always argued for Henry's because it was cheaper. "Think of Mom," he said. "She doesn't have much money." But I never thought of Mom; I thought of myself.

We lived in town now. Townies. Central City (population 1,000). I couldn't have been happier. It was a place out of an unwritten storybook entitled *Twilight of Small-Town, America.* Mom had signed a contract to teach junior high language arts at Linn-Mar, in Marion. She would have to commute.

It was April. I walked to school taking River Street; on my left, sturdy wooden houses shaded by huge oaks and maples. In one of those houses lived the Steele family. Brett and Squeak Steele, a basketball star, were becoming good friends. Squeak had two brothers and two sisters; all smart, all athletes, all strong Catholics. His mother was a school janitor, and his father had hung himself in the family garage. I never passed the garage without thinking of how Squeak had found him dangling. A mortal sin. Everyone knew the story, but no one ever asked a Steele about it. The father had worked for the railroad, and embezzled money, and the railroad had discovered the missing funds. Alongside me, on my right, ran the Wapsipinicon, which divided the town. As I crossed the bridge, the morning sun glinted on the dark-green ripples like lost fish. On the opposite bank, more maples and the town's wading pool, which waited for June and its leggy lifeguard, Mary Carley, who watched the kiddies and stopped traffic with her blonde good looks. Mary would die at age 16 in a car driven by her boyfriend when it collided with a train. The prettiest girl in high school. The long, straight highway stretch outside of town, where kids opened the throttle of their motorbikes or floored the accelerators of their cars. Mary's father, one of the volunteer ambulance men, responded to the accident scene. Her funeral was held in the high school gym. The casket open. Mary lay in her cheerleading black-and-red sweater and black culottes. Her face heavily made up–almost orange. I stood over her grave many times in the lifetime since. The girl who surely would have been homecoming queen, her grave older than my grandmother's. The girl whose life was cut short. Grass already growing over the headstone.

⁂

I had been freed of the farm's tyranny. Pristine streets, the light from the blue sky sifting from leaves. I walked over the bridge and then stopped on Main Street at Snyder's Grocery and bought a bag of Cheetos, a Kit Kat, and a Mounds, or it might have been a $100,000 Bar. I ate them all on the way to school. I picked up the twins, Penny and Jenny Dake. Our threesome marched up Main Street, past Sauer's Jack-N-Jill, Carpenter's Beauty Salon, Lawrence's Funeral Home, Don & Dick's Standard, and finally, Norton's Drug Store, with its old-fashioned soda counter. Norton's was my after-school stop for ice-cream sundaes and root beer floats. I was running track, so I didn't gain weight. The sun split the budding leaves into green shadows. How unspoiled this jewel of a town was just before interstates and strip malls and big-box stores blew it all away.

No one knows what is coming, although Vietnam is siphoning off the high school boy graduates not marked for college. The Lottery. Three hundred and sixty-six blue plastic capsules with birthdates inside them are plucked from a glass container. It's the order of call for all men between the ages of 18 and 26. The first capsule picked contains the birthdates assigned the number 1. My brother Joel's number is 3. Even if he is in college, he is sure to go to Vietnam. Florence will support his decision to go to Canada if that is what he decides. She did not raise a son to become cannon fodder. He enlists in the National Guard, deferring his military service until he graduates from college. My junior year I write to a soldier serving in Khe Sanh. I tell him about the class play I'm acting in and the International Order of the Rainbow for good teenage girls I belong to. I send him a photo and a box of cookies. He mails me back a photo of himself, half of the picture cut away. His short black hair matches his sunglasses. His skin is preternaturally tan, the color of baking brick, yet the red-purple hickeys on his neck stand out like a bleed of wild flowers. I can make out the couch he's sitting on, his right arm lopped off at the shoulder. Though he's tried to erase her, I can see the shoulder and arm of the long-haired bar girl with red lips.

⁂

The walk to school shows off your popularity. Girlfriends pair up with boyfriends, everyone pairs up with someone. I munch candy bars and keep a lookout for the junior and senior guys on motorcycles, the farm kids in their second-hand pickups cruising in from the country. Everything I see is *town.* Here, Ronnie Simmen can pick me up on his motorcycle, drive to the deserted fairgrounds, and park in the livestock-judging arena. In a stall for the 4-H prize cows and pigs, we slide off the motorcycle, and Ronnie, in his starched jeans and green shirt with salmon stripes, pulls me to him. (Now I see Ronnie Simmen on Facebook. Through all that time and space. He and his Thai wife are still happily married. An Air Force pilot, he had met her in Southeast Asia.)

Living in town, I can come and go to after-school activities, such as play practice and chorus and marching band. My flute-playing is so abysmal that the band director asks if I'd like to be a pom-pom girl. I'm thrilled. (Florence refuses to ever watch me kick my legs in the air. I'm as frivolous as she is serious.) I'm running the half-mile and becoming friends with Cynthia Howe. The smart, strong-willed girl I am so drawn to. I remember Al saying about Central City, "The Howe brothers run this town." And Cynthia's father is Delwin Howe.

Then Al tried to reclaim my mother. I should have said to myself, *Think of Mom.* Instead, I'd shuddered when I learned that Bluebeard of the Sticks wanted a reconciliation. He asked us to give him another chance and return to his farm. His blue truck pulled into the apartment's parking lot. I saw him through the barely curtained sliding glass door of the apartment; there was no regular door. He wanted Florence to spend Saturday night at the farm. To talk. She agreed. He stood at the door in his farmer overalls. His ball cap like a kettle on his head. His black waders jingling with buckles.

I am ashamed to admit my callousness toward my mother. I was a town girl now; I won't, won't, won't go back to the farm. Florence left with him, got into the blue truck. Since the honeymoon, he'd never driven his car, always the truck. She stayed the night at the gray farmhouse. What if Brett and I had already graduated; if it had just been the two of them? Then if Al came for her in his truck, she might have moved back in. She would have escaped being alone. I feared moving back to his farm. The terrible place where I could go nowhere without a car, back to the icy bedroom upstairs, the sloping roof, the coal heat, piglets for Sunday dinner; the place where no one could possibly be happy.

The next time I see them together, they are standing at the sliding door. Al's half in and half out in his chore clothes and his hat, and he is kissing her. Her face reaches up to him. And I blurt out, "Mom, you said you'd never kiss him again."

And with those words, I shame her and chase him away.

Now, my older self judges my younger self harshly. I think of the story I had heard for the first time in Florence's last years. "Oh, I don't know if I want to tell you this, but my sister and I were both going to Coe College. I looked up to Aunt Patsy in those days. She knew the ropes. I was dating someone I met while sitting in the library with my music books. Dwayne sat down and wrote his name in my songbook. We started to date. But Aunt Patsy and her boyfriend didn't like him. One weekend when Dwayne went home, they talked me into going out with a red-haired fella, a friend of theirs, and he kissed me goodnight. As soon as Dwayne got back, they went to him with the story of the kiss and broke us up. I was from the country. I didn't know any better."

I was like my aunt–betraying her kiss.

Stones Aren't Deaf

I walk into the room on the fourth day of my mother's dying and realize that there will be no more groaning, no more grabbing the iron bars of the bed, no more flailing as if sinking and flying. No more of Florence fighting off those who touch her, fighting the blood pressure machine's harmless Velcro wrapped around her upper arm. The drugs have settled her into a comatose state. Joel is visiting the lawyers, trying to make a last-minute save on some monies. I'm here, waiting for Hospice.

Matt, who will lead my mother to the door of death, knocks lightly. He is the Hospice nurse/caseworker assigned to Florence. He had met her a week ago, when she was still walking around. Joel said that she had latched onto Matt and hugged him as if he were her own son. Our mother, who held herself aloof from the physical, who was uncomfortable with touch, is, at this late hour, hanging onto others, hugging and holding, clutching for human warmth. Matt is of medium height, with pale blue eyes behind glasses, brown hair, and a soft mustache. A stethoscope hangs from his neck. He wears a shoulder bag, and in it are thermometers and gauzes and blood pressure Velcro, and more pamphlets, and a thick notebook. The Book of the Dead. He speaks in a well-modulated, soothing tone. I find myself nodding at his words; his voice is hypnotic. He tells me, as Shauna, the weekend Hospice nurse did, what wisdom the Hospice booklet contains. "Remember that, although she appears not to respond, your mother may be able to hear everything you say."

"But she doesn't have her hearing aids in," I say. She is deaf as a stone, but perhaps stones aren't deaf either. Not if everything in Creation is animated with life.

"Would you feel more comfortable if they were in?" he asks.

I don't know what to answer. "No, she took them off for sleeping. I think she would prefer not having them in." But what would her choice be?

"Now that the brain has cut off her vision, her hearing could be more acute," Matt says. He takes and records her vital signs.

There is some lag in the seconds between her breaths; then, normal breathing. Matt pinches her skin. Tenting is starting. The skin doesn't relax back; he shows me how it stays peaked on her forearm. I think of my father's Boy Scout tent and sleeping outside in it on a sultry farm night under the oak. In the moonlight, leaf-shadow on the canvas took on the shape of sickles and raised arms. The Grim Reaper. Things are moving now; fluids are flowing to the core. Her extremities will turn purple as the blood travels to the heart and lungs and brain. The brain is fighting at all costs to protect itself. I've never felt so much respect for the body. All the cells and systems that live independent of us, our skin and blood and pumping heart, our lungs, the great god brain.

What is going on inside her? What thought fragments? Delirium. What happens? She is not sure who is surrounding the bed; not sure where the bed is. How she is dressed to be in country school, to be walking the roads in her gray dress; cold, then hot. The one room. Now she remembers they have ten cows, that her father is good with animals, that he works hard, that people no longer know what it is to work hard with the body. She keeps walking the school road, and it must be during one of the bad years, when money has dried up across the land. But now she thinks it's not so bad.

At home we always have milk, farmer's cheese made with the cloth sling, buttermilk, heavy cream. All the beautiful things her father's cow gives.

The aides walking in and out of my mother's room stop to talk. Ashley, the curious aide, says, "Isn't Florence your grandmother, not your mother?" I tell her that Florence is my mother, that she had me at age 40. "I could have had a child every year if I'd allowed it," she had told me, almost bragging. "My body was that healthy." I have hours to pass beside my mother's bed before Joel relieves me, but I don't feel the need for relief. I am grateful to be here. Glad. No one else will know that at my beginning, when I dropped my baby bottle, my mother had said, "Stephy, your bottle broke. Now you'll have to drink from a cup." And I took the cup and drank.

I long blamed her for making me believe I wasn't person enough to be treated the way real people were. When the day came that I would run, I was 18 and of age, an adult in name only. I understand now the harried Florence trying to raise three children, teach, and only on one day for a few hours give herself over to Hilda, the gravel road beautician, to feel the sluice of warm water and strong, freckled fingers rubbing her scalp, massaging in the shampoo, then a waterfall of rinsing. "Oh, that's so relaxing," I'd heard her say during a shampoo, in almost a moan. That word meant birdsong and warm summer mornings with absolutely nothing you *had* to do. That was *relaxing.*

And it was on the last day of my September visit that a schoolteacher friend called from Texas. Florence answered. Her phone, with its amplification, had been created especially for the hard of hearing. After pleasantries, my mother turned to me, mouthing, whispering, "I can't think of anything to say!" There was terror in her face. She made a fist and hit her head with it. "Mom, Mom, it's okay! Just say yes agreeably and let her talk."

Yet, three months before her death, she wrote this:

"I'm wondering if your choice of New York City as a place to 'start' was a mistake–an overcrowded place, containing too many 'searching' people. You have so much intelligence and such a variety of 'ability.' You should be at the 'head' of things."

⁂

I sit on the bed in the room next to Florence's and go through a shoebox of photographs–sepia and black-and-white. I open the window to let in the warm night breath. As a girl on the farm, I had absorbed my grandmother's tales of old tragedies. All the family ghosts have been left to my care. After me, there will be no one to remember them.

I hold a sepia card and study my great-aunt and great-uncle's wedding photograph, taken over a century ago. From under the camera's hood, the photographer peers at them as he fuses their faces into a sepia eternity.

I touch the card. Reid's Studio is where they stand in their wedding attire. My great-aunt Josie's shoulder presses Great-uncle Joseph's. The bride and maid-of-honor wear Victorian collars and starched white dresses of whalebone and hook. Mutton-leg sleeves. Their net gloves hold long-stemmed roses. Like beautiful dreams you hear in your inner ear. The groom and best man's solemn faces shine above their stiff collars and suits pressed by flat irons. The bride and best man are sister and brother; the groom and maid-of-honor are brother and sister–the wedding party complete. Their bodies–except for their faces and the men's ungloved hands–remain hidden, like humid hyacinth.

Teenagers, virgins all. The best man, John Telecky, will marry the maid-of-honor, Emily Buresh, and they will become my maternal grandparents. The blue-eyed/dark-haired foursome has movie-star looks. I know each of their fates, yet I try to read what their gazes say. Not one shows teeth, and only the bride has what might be a lip smile on her mouth, while the groom's hand looks shy, self-conscious.

The children of Czech immigrants, my grandfather fell in love with my grandmother when she was 12 years old and singing in the church choir. This generation of Czechs marries Czechs, and look no farther than the pews of its country church for mates. The bride has known the groom all her life–the quietest boy in her Sunday school.

I calculate 1905 as the year of the wedding. The new 20th Century takes its terrible baby steps. The Great War has not yet happened, although rumblings between the European Alliances can be heard. The rumblings aren't heard here, not this far into the heartland. Iowa. I try to envision a world before rural electricity and flush toilets and running water, where my people chore from dawn to dusk. The Somme, the Russian Revolution, the Armenian Genocide; none of it has happened. Neither have antibiotics, nor polio vaccinations, nor television. And, on the farm, workhorses plow furrows. Horses carry the loads; the dark blue beasts are seven-hands-tall in their fetlocks and bridles. Florence has told me that my forebears never shot their workhorses or sold them for meat when they got too old to plow. Man and beast forged unbreakable bonds under a boiling Midwestern sun. Much loved, the gentle giants were let out to pasture, having earned their rest a thousand times over.

While Great-uncle Joseph's face reminds me of a young Paul Newman, his hands are already knotted from farm work. I picture the four of them leaving the studio and riding back to the bride's father's farm in a horse and buggy. Perhaps they stop to eat raspberries, ripening along the road under a haze of dust. Joseph cleans the fruit with his tongue before offering it to his bride. Looking at her, he thinks, *she is mine.* Her eyes answer, *I am heat lightning.* They both laugh. Raspberries. Just-picked fruit.

For a wedding present, Josie and Joseph are given land and a farmhouse. I'd been told by my grandmother that hard work is how they lived. This generation of women can plant and weed, sew, pickle sauerkraut, wash clothes using scrub boards, fill cookstoves with cobs. They're strong as windbreak trees. They make bread for the week. They knead the dough, throw and pound it with the heels of their hands, they pick up the ax and guillotine the hen, pluck the boiled feathers. I believe Josie does all this gladly. *Hers. He is hers.*

Great-uncle Joseph fathers four children before his 34th year. My great-aunt gives birth to them in the same bed in which they were conceived. It is 1918, and spring-planting time, when he goes into a field to dynamite a stump, the tree itself already cut and used to repair the barn. Alone, he packs the gunpowder around the base of the stump and lights the fuse. He runs for cover. That part of the tree left alive aims a splinter into his brain. Josie finds him in the field. Does she try to drag him to the house, or hold what is left of his head in her lap and think of those raspberries? Does she leave the young ones, saddle a horse, and ride for help? William, Joanna, Esther, Edwin. Two in country school and two at home the day their father goes into the field with the dynamite.

He'll leave behind a wife so in love with him she'll never marry again. "I won't let another man raise his children," she says. My great-grandfather, a gruff and forbidding man, takes his weeping daughter on his lap and rocks her. "It hurts so much," she cries. At 9 years old, her eldest son, William, becomes a man.

My grandmother told me how Josie and her four children had survived the Depression, when corn sold for 2 cents a bushel. All five of them worked the farm, and the Buresh and Telecky families helped. Yet, of the two couples in the wedding photo, all four children of my maternal grandparents graduated from college, three going on to obtain postgraduate degrees, while only one of Josie's children went to college; the other three graduated from school to the fields. Esther, the youngest, had married at 16. Then, as now, a household headed by a single woman was often poorer, with fewer opportunities for her offspring.

Great-aunt Josie's years of hardship had passed before I was born. She'd reached her late 70s and was comfortable in a small house with red-frame porch windows, across the gravel road from the farm where her son Edwin lived with his family. I was enamored of her ears; the pierced lobes and bits of blue glass that dangled there. The other women in my family wore clunky clip-on earrings. Her eyes were pale blue and, in her old age, their luminosity had not dimmed. I couldn't ask my elders questions like, *do you still remember your husband* or *do you miss your own impossible beauty*? My great-uncle must have loved looking at her as he drank his farmer's coffee from the blue-speckled pot, even after four children. *Pullet,* he may have called her. *Soft one.*

Farm women, whose hearts are strong, die hard. Great-aunt Josie deserved an easy death but suffered bone cancer and lost a leg to gangrene. Did she wonder if her husband would come for her, now that she was wrinkled and hobbled, one-legged? Did she recall the shudder of her first married night? I hope when she met him in the tunnel of light, she was once again a girl, all bloom and fruited tomato, running wild seed. *Beloved,* she might call out in her death haze as she passed the garden she fed her young children from, trailing the corn and its veiling silk, the squash vines snaking through dirt, with blossoms like top cream.

Joseph's funeral took place on the front lawn of the Buresh farmhouse. Because she had been so young then, now my mother can't remember anything but how green the grass was.

The wedding photograph moment had lain dormant in my grandmother's picture drawer through World War I, World War II, the Holocaust, Korea, Sputnik, Vietnam, and the Cold War, until, at her death, it passed into my mother's hands, and now into mine. I have no one to pass the relic on to, and at my death, the moment will die too.

I must make the picture live.

Rabbit Trap

Joel and I are called into the Village Ridge office, where Diane, the no-nonsense manager, conducts business. The retirement franchise's headquarters is in Denver, and Joel tells me that when the Colorado bigwigs are on the premises, Diane turns demure and obliging. Otherwise, behind her banker's solid oak desk, she is the decider. Whether it's a change in the seating chart of the dining room where residents are assigned tables, or a stopped-up toilet, Diane has the say-so. She's a slender baby boomer; dark, wavy hair to her shoulders, in a long-sleeved green knit top and fitted jeans. Iowa conducts much of its business in casual clothes.

My mother dislikes women, especially younger ones, and here is a younger woman (relative to her age) who is able to tell her what to do. "Oh, that woman at the head. She thinks she knows everything!" Florence can no longer remember names, so Diane is *that head woman* or simply *that woman.* No amount of anger or refusal will change Diane's mind. Her voice is pitched low like a smoker's, almost a whiskey voice. There's a wariness in her expression, watchfulness; how the eyes become when they supervise other people. "That head woman, I don't like her," Florence often told me.

Diane is well-versed in Joel. In March, when he was visiting, Florence could not be reasoned with, and he lost his temper and yelled at her. "I've always been able to talk with Mom on a logical level," he explained. "But this time I couldn't. She would not stop beating up on herself. 'Oh, I'm no good. This dumb head! You don't know how it is to be old. Nobody wants you. I can't remember anything!'" The deaf residents were, miraculously, able to hear Joel's raised voice. They suspected elder abuse and reported it to Diane, who called him into her office to discuss the incident.

Nurse Laura, a registered nurse and staff supervisor, sits opposite Diane. Straight hair clasped at her nape, brownish, but a muted brown that almost appears gray. Not a dry salt-and-pepper gray, but fine and shiny. She is not old, perhaps late 30s or early 40s, so this gray must have been the color of even her baby hair. Unusual too are her eyes; large, deep-set gray eyes, the color of charcoal mixed with fog. Yet, penetrating eyes. They do not allow you to examine her; you are forced to look away. She is heavy. Perhaps two hundred and eighty pounds, perhaps three hundred. When my mother broke her elbow last August, it was Nurse Laura who insisted that her arm be recast after Florence bent the uncomfortable thumb piece off. "I can't stand it," she had objected. "I just can't stand my thumb like that." A hard loop of plastic encircled her thumb and anchored the elbow. "Stephanie, it's hard as wood. Why would that big woman put this animal on me?" Nurse Laura would not relent. Her face is intelligent, but her overseer eyes are vigilant like Diane's. She wears a muumuu and a white nurse's jacket, and from her neck, a stethoscope hangs.

"She is angry. Wouldn't you be?" Joel remarked about Nurse Laura last night. "Everywhere she goes, people look and judge. She's become hateful."

You sometimes become twisted when you carry the burden of flesh.

"That nurse is so bossy and large, she can't wear regular clothes. She wears nightgowns," said my mother, who rarely criticized anyone for being overweight. But these were the women who had taken her mailbox keys away and changed her place in the dining room to a corner table, although they had, of course, done it for Florence's own good.

With them, she could not cover her ears with her hands to block the sound of their voices, as she sometimes did with me.

Diane tells us that Joel and I are welcome to eat our meals in the cafeteria. "But we don't allow any drinking or smoking in the room," she cautions. "We had a family here a month ago who had problems with drinking. Laura, remember the Franklins?"

Laura nods. "Yes, the Franklins."

"And every four hours the aides will come into the room to turn and change your mother," Diane continues. "When that happens, you will be asked to leave the room."

"Now, why would we need to leave the room?" Joel asks.

"They'll be changing your mother's adult diaper," Nurse Laura answers.

"My sister and I prefer to be with our mother when the aides come in," my brother says, with an air of finality.

Diane sidesteps the brewing confrontation and asks if we've made arrangements with a funeral home. My brother tells her we've selected Stewart-Campbell, although Florence will not be embalmed, as her body is being donated to the University of Iowa's School of Anatomy. It was her choice for decades to be a living organ donor, and she always carried her card, but since then, she's decided to deed her whole body. Nothing would be wasted.

"What percentage of residents who die here donate their bodies to science?" Joel, ever the avid questioner, inquires.

Diane leans forward over her desk. "Your mother's the first to give her body."

That satisfies Joel. Florence, convinced of the body's resurrection, holds no sentimentality about the worn-out container. And a funeral? "What does it matter after I'm dead?" she'd said.

I hope the body-donation people, when they see this almost 99-year-old woman, with her thick brown hair and half-inch of white at the hairline, treat her with respect. I hope they will not say, like one of the aides did last night while turning her, "Needs a dye job." I should have risen up from my chair in outrage, but Florence had schooled me well in being pleasant to strangers. I smiled along with them. "Yes, she needs to get her hair color done," I'd agreed.

A month ago, I had reminded my brothers to see about getting her hair colored. Florence had taken care of that herself until the last two months of her life. Why had the aide sneered *she needs a dye job* in front of me? Why didn't I say something? Brown hair on Florence showed her spunk, her unwillingness to fade away. Will those who receive the body when she is no longer a mother but a cadaver treat her with respect, or will they joke and sneer?

We are dismissed.

* *

I press the code to open the side door of the Memory Care Unit and step into a small, fenced-in courtyard. Flowers border the circular asphalt, pansies and gladiolas lick the humid air with their furry tongues. In my lap, some of Florence's most recent letters–those she had received and those she had tried to write. Evidence, in her own handwriting, that her mind was fragmenting. Disintegrating.

Six months ago, she had received the carefully folded two-page missive I'm reading; it is from a former student who attended the Iowa Braille and Sight Saving School, where Florence had taught dramatics and speech. These were the years immediately after my father's death, when I lived with my grandparents on the farm. Florence and my brothers rented a small house in Vinton, Iowa, two blocks from the Braille School; the massive 19th Century academic buildings and dormitories sprawled under 100-year-old oaks. Florence took my brothers (and me, when I visited) there on Saturdays when she went to correct papers. Cornmeal-colored limestone housed the desks with raised surfaces, the tunnels that connected all the buildings, the hand railings lining the halls like the silk webbing of spiders. In the high-ceilinged rooms, there were topographic maps with mountain ranges and canyons, and globes with the names of countries and cities in raised dots that felt like poppy seeds. I would close my eyes and visualize being blind. I pretended that I, too, lived in an unending twilight, because gray, not black, is the color of the universe when you're blind.

I hear a pounding on the glass door behind me. I turn and see the woman who screams at night. "Open the door," she says. "I want to go outside." Her ruddy face, square and large, her hair cut like a medieval page's, seems to be there only to support her black-frame glasses with thick lenses, behind which her widened eyes appear huge, as if they are blue planets where all the landscape has vanished.

"I'm sorry," I tell her, "but I can't let you out." There is such urgency in her voice. I picture my grandfather's box trap with its wooden lid that shut as soon as the rabbit scurried inside for the bait. This woman knows how it feels inside the splintery box. Trapped.

"Let me out. Please," she wails, until an aide comes and takes her away.

When my mother received the letter, she read it to me slowly over the phone. Her former student's name is Joyce, and she remembered my mother with great fondness. She and her future husband, Robert, had performed in the high school plays that Florence directed. Joyce never forgot how much she had enjoyed them, and how excellent my mother's direction had been. They were the high point of Joyce's school years. Now there would be a fifty-year class reunion in Des Moines, and the entire class wanted my mother to attend as guest of honor. In telling me, Florence laughed with delight. “I could never, never go. Now let me read you the rest.”

“I’m listening,” I said.

She had to pause, and then struggle, as if each word weighed as much as a limestone block that she had to carry on her tongue and drop before picking up another. Many words, lifting and dropping. She fought to sound out the syllables. If will were all it took, her will would have forced the paragraphs out of her synapses. Her memory played hide-and-seek with the alphabet. Did she remember the Braille script? The raised dots in cells of up to six dots; the *a*, a single dot; *x*, four dots, one above the other.

“Mom, keep reading,” I said when she stopped.

Yes, she found the words when she went slowly. Her former blind students were happily married and had two sighted children. The boy was a social worker, and the girl, an engineer.

“Don’t you think it was nice of them to write?” Florence had asked again.

Was she back in the past, coaching the blind actors as they read from the script with their fingertips? Their skin absorbing the Irish brogue of Eugene O’Neill’s characters. Lips moving as their fingers journeyed from dot to dot. Royal-blue velvet curtains parted on opening night and the house lights went down. A real theater, holding hundreds of velveteen seats, and all of them filled. I was in one of them, a 5-year-old girl with big ears. Taking in the mystery and beauty of those voices rising in the darkened theater.

It took her a week to answer that letter, whereas her sentences (sometimes abrasive ones) used to fly off her pen or typewriter with alacrity. She agonized, copying the paragraphs over when she found errors after reading it again aloud on the phone to her children. When I think of that schoolteacher’s struggle to write the letter, I see it as the most ferocious battle of her life; she was composing her very last correspondence. Although she would never brag, her writing had voice and style; her language, rich and colorful. Her penmanship highly legible, in the way that few of my generation can boast. To say nothing of the *thumb generation*, which is losing the ability to write in longhand altogether.

She had stopped writing me two- and three-page letters the year before. I began saving the envelopes she sent with only the Anchor House devotional pamphlets inside. Her envelopes used to be stuffed with newspaper clippings and her suggestions for bettering my life. Now her notes were written on pieces of scratch paper left over from her teaching days; spelling lists on one side in mimeograph blue, and on the other side, phrases or single words. "Mistake." "Maybe Stephanie and Joel can sell my jewelry." "Is there some way I can give Stephanie my left arm?"

I witnessed this. Still, I did not think *dementia.*

Dementia. You can die of it, not just stew in it as it uproots you from your memories. It is the death before death. My great-uncle Frank was the only relative I saw who suffered that death before death. No Memory Care Unit for him. Great-aunt Anna took care of him. They lived on a small farm while his arteries hardened and he hallucinated.

Great-uncle Frank had worked as a tinner at the meatpacking plant before Wilson's bought it. A tinner, one of those long-gone occupations, and so he worked with sheet metal and, from my mother's stories, was a hypochondriac, always certain that his cold would bloom into pneumonia, that the pain in his side would turn into appendicitis, yet he never complained when Florence and her brothers lived with them as they went through high school.

Great-aunt Anna would invite us to Sunday dinner, my brothers and mother and grandmother. I loved Sundays at the small farm that was tucked into the woods just two miles from Cedar Rapids. My great-aunt and grandmother belonged to the generation of women, the last self-sufficient ones in America, who worked from the time they got up until they went to bed. They were perfectionists. My grandmother ended up with more land, farmhouses, and bank accounts because she'd married a land-owning farmer, while Aunt Anna wed a man who worked for a wage. Anna had been the apple of her mother's eye, while Emily, my grandmother, was her father's favorite. I realize how good it is to recall these details that make up a family mythology, before death sweeps it all away.

I don't want to forget how the Rambler would pull into the dirt driveway and park in the grass by the chicken coop–gray-shingled and without a fence. My brothers and I would burst from the back seat. The Leghorn hens and strawberry-red roosters pecked the warm dirt for worms and bugs. The sun on my face was filled with their clucking. Behind us, the stately barn that held grain was rented by the neighboring farmer. Its doors were padlocked.

The house's front porch faced the road; the side porch, the outhouse. Aunt Anna's little house had no indoor plumbing. I used the outhouse, which my aunt kept pristine. The sun broke through pinholes in the roof. No toilet paper; instead, catalog pages had been folded for use. Sears washing machines, cotton briefs, shirt dresses, and Nehru collars. Wasps love dung, and built their papery nests in the rafter corners. I listened to the sound of my pee falling through the air like rain, the drops hitting the Summer Sale pages shipwrecked at the pit's bottom. There were two holes in the gray wood, and I wondered if two people had ever sat together here. I thought of winters in Iowa.

Sunday dinner at Aunt Anna's, we entered the house through the side porch, where Red, the Irish Setter, slept. A beautiful burnt-orange dog, he guarded the old couple, although he was old himself. Inside, no running water, but everything was immaculate; the massive oak table with scrolled legs, the starched lace curtains. The kitchen smelled of its two stoves, a chicken baking in the gas stove's oven and, on the cast-iron cookstove, a five-gallon kettle of water boiling potatoes. I was in awe of the cookstove, as if it were an ancient beast preening itself, proud of its six burners and firebox. The stove had a flue and an ash pan, a winter and summer firebox. A complicated, lost technology. Its perfume–the scent of struck kitchen matches.

Aunt Anna's only child lived in town but hauled canisters of fresh water here in his Jeep and chopped firewood in the slough across the road for his parents.

Even on warm Sundays, the cookstove would be lit. Without its heat, Uncle Frank shivered in his dementia winter. "You really had to have the knack," my mother once said, "to make a meal on an old-fashioned cookstove and to bake kolaches. Everything burns easily. The temperature is never the same." The old Czech women knew how to cook with fire. I heard stories of my great-grandfather Buresh, who would bring guests home for dinner and surprise my great-grandmother. Nothing rattled her. She would pick up the ax, go to the hen house and wring a chicken's neck, chop off its head, boil the chicken outside in the iron kettle to soften the feathers; then pluck it, cut the bird apart, and pull out the intestines, the liver, and grit bag; bake it in a cookstove, and soon have a juicy chicken on the table between bowls of dumplings and sauerkraut.

Although the arms of my great-aunt and grandmother had long ago lost their muscle, they were titans who could lug and chop, plant and can, butcher and bake like angels. Both women's thumbs were crisscrossed with knife scars. Anna had straight, silken hair, and Emily, outrageously kinky hair. Women of their generation never cut or dyed their hair; they wore it up, off their faces, braided or bunned. Where did Emily's hair come from? No one else in the family had it. Perhaps it came from some truly primeval ancestor.

My grandmother set the pan of kolaches she'd brought onto the table. She put on an apron and started to help. This was her sister's kitchen and each prepared the Czech dishes their own way. Anna's cucumbers had more cream and less onion, her pickled beets more vinegar; her sauerkraut was boiled longer and came out browner; her dumplings, not fluffy. Both ways were delicious. Anna's marzipan cookies were exotic almond-paste islands. Her meringue, bites of sweet clouds.

I drank from the pale green glass; I found it hard to decide between that and the apricot-colored one. The cold water from the refrigerator tasted better in the green glass, as though swallowing through a willow wand. "Wash your hands," Mother said. There was a pump in the kitchen sink, and I worked the handle until ground water splashed into a silver pan. The formal dining room, opened only for company, smelled of dates and figs and hidden buffet drawers, the mustiness inside a sterling silver chest.

After the dinner dishes were done, Anna and Emily visited in the parlor while Uncle Frank napped. One sat in the rocker and another in a chair. In Czech and English they spoke of childhood friends and relatives, the genealogy of who married whom, and who died, who was sick. All the missing people of their lives. Their voices rose and fell, and then went silent. I looked up and saw them staring out the window into the field. The past must be there, I thought.

I took out the stereoscope and the tin box filled with sepia cards, and slid the thick card into the prongs that held the dual image in front of the face mask embedded with three-dimensional lenses. I disappeared into the sepia past. I time-traveled to the 19th Century, where men with furry mustaches stood in a rubble of rock. Some leaned on picks and shovels; others clutched sticks of dynamite. All wore long underwear and suspenders. They were dynamiting a railroad bridge through a mountain. I entered the Edwardian parlor of a big-game hunter. It was a room crowded with sudden death. There were heads of lions, jaguars, hyenas, tigers, and rhinoceroses mounted on the floral-patterned walls, snakeskins and alligators' pelts, stuffed owls and crocodiles. Bear rugs stretched over the polished wood floors between enormous vases of pampas grass. Every lamp fringed, a doily on every surface. I visited Victorian girls in white tulip frocks who played with china dolls in identical white frocks. I saw the Spanish-American War's Rough Riders. Warhorses, in all their solemnity. Hobos. Black men in bowler hats roasting a possum over a campfire, watermelon rinds and chicken bones scattered over the ground. One man strummed a banjo. The card identified them as *darkies*.

The sisters' recipes that now lie in the coffin with them. Emily in Rogers' Grove with the Teleckys. Anna in Buresh Cemetery, where she is close to her beloved mother. "Oh, my grandmother Josephine," Florence said, "would bridle the horse, hitch the wagon, and ride over to see Aunt Anna. She was like a man. Afraid of nothing." One thing she did fear–the English language. Josephine, who was born in Iowa, had never learned to speak English, while her husband, born in Bohemia, had.

Moonlight Mile

I am sitting beside my mother's bed. My mother is now breathing in the Cheyne-Stokes pattern, her hands at her sides. Harsh, snoring-like breaths that stop for seconds and then start. The respiratory system is detaching itself; the signals from the brain are starting to fade. Her diaphragm is working harder. The body itself is fragmenting. Entropy. I want her to know I am here. That I would give much to erase our troubled past. I stand up and press my lips to her forehead. Her dying smells of Moonlight Mile body lotion from Bed, Bath & Beyond. Her last hair-coloring like a sand painting, the chlorine level of water; the turquoise separated from the brown.

Matt, the Hospice coordinator, and his assistant are in the hall giving instructions to Angie, the in-charge nurse. They'll be leaving the Memory Care Unit and moving on to visit other patients in Marion.

I can kiss and hold my mother all I want now. I press my lips to her forehead again. I hold her hand and then lift its bigness to my cheek. Her fingers still strong, never stiff with arthritis. All my life I've wanted to hug and kiss her, but touch made her so uncomfortable. Perhaps she needed to stay strong and angry. Giving in to touch and softness might reveal weakness or too much pain. Then, too, there was my past.

•• ••

In my mother's cedar chest, where her treasured wedding dress lies (in that storage lot), is a photograph of me. I'm wearing ripped blue jeans and twine belt and wire-rims and a white see-through top, and I am bra-less. This photo my mother would not allow me to throw away. "That is mine," she said. To show me, to show me the monster I had been. I was home from my first summer in Canada, still 17, about to turn 18. I'd gone there to work in a Christian Missionary Alliance Camp, but I'd left after a month. I took off for Toronto and Ottawa and Montreal, where I would meet Michael. I first saw him on St. Catherine Street, near the stone church on whose dirt lawn the long-haired panhandlers and transients gathered with their sleeping bags. In a turtleneck and bell-bottom jeans, his black hair tangled down his back to his waist, the longest hair I'd ever seen on a male. To me, he was dazzling. Seeing him, my mother's red pencil would have underlined the word *repulsive.* We slept next to each other in the hostel like a brother and sister. When I stretched out beside him on the floor, I smelled his hair full of leaves and smoke. I inhaled the same fields I grew up with. What would it be like to sleep outside, his long torso silvered with moonlight, the Big Dipper pouring its stars on us?

When I returned home at the end of summer with a backpack, Florence asked, "Where are your suitcases and the nice clothes you left with?" I answered, "I gave them away. That's all there is, man." My mother wrote my words down. "You dumped the bag in the kitchen and went around the corner into your room. I saw demons."

I picture myself under an overpass in Montreal with Michael, our thumbs out. The boots I was wearing gave me blisters, so I stepped out of them. A car stopped and we ran to it, the expensive boots left behind.

⁂

"Hey, kiddo," Joel says from the doorway. "Look who I found wandering the halls."

He has driven to the country to pick up Florence's cousin from her farm, only a stone's throw from the Telecky acreage where we grew up. He is standing in the hall, talking to Matt, while Betty Skalsky, with her pale Irish skin, her curly white hair, and lilting voice thumps into the room on her walker. Betty's husband, Eugene, was Florence's first cousin. I hug her large, doughy body, which smells of the Skalsky farmhouse. Joel has said the Skalskys are millionaires, and yet the linoleum in their kitchen is still the same ripped brown checkerboard we walked on as kids. They have held on to the land as though a religion: worship of the black soil deity. I think of the pig valve that was implanted some years ago in Betty's 83-year-old heart. Joel tells Betty that when he was alone with Mother, he tried to wake her. He does not specify what he tried, but he could not reach her–she has slipped beyond us. Betty glances at my mother, then turns away. Perhaps it is too hard for her, knowing that this is the way of all flesh, especially her own.

Betty wants to talk to me, so we sit in the patients' kitchen and share granola flakes and milk. I do not have to tell her about New York or my life, as she shows no interest in hearing about them. I only have to ask how she is, and the details spill out. "I'm not a spring chicken anymore, and after my heart operation, they found cancer. It seems they cut the cancer out of my bowel, and I haven't had any problems since. Steven and Shay bought a Winnebago for my great grandson. Animal's living where the Minors used to." She chatters on about Steven, her only child; Shay, her only grandchild; and her only great-grandchild, Animal, whose birth name is Kevin but who has gone by his nickname since grade school. A decade ago, I didn't recognize Steven at the Buresh/Telecky reunion–weathered, the gristle of gray whiskers clinging to his cheeks. Steven is known to speak to his mother in a way that my brothers never did to Florence. Betty loves to talk, and if she lets out too much chatter, Steven will say, "Old woman, shut up or we'll bury you next to Big." Big, a favorite horse, is buried in the back pasture. Yet, Steven guided the farm to impossible prosperity.

We stroll back into my mother's room and Betty takes a chair with her back to my mother. Betty, a nurse as well as a farmer's wife, married Florence's cousin, the prickly Eugene, whose personality was as cantankerous as the donkey, Jack's. It was a mixed marriage–Betty, Irish, and Eugene, Czech. In an intensely religious extended family, the Skalsky branch seemed immune to the pleasures of church. Eugene found fault with everything: the ground he walked on and the air he breathed, from his Dubek neighbors to the impoverished hired man and his delinquent children. He distrusted the government and evangelists. His bitching made hilarious commentary. He tore the clay feet out from under the golden idols. Only after Betty's death would we learn that Eugene, following a two-week hospital stay, after a week of kindness toward his wife and son unlike anything they'd known before, stood up from the table and said he intended to die in the bed he was born in. He went upstairs, got in the antique bed where his mother had given birth to him, where his son had been conceived, where he and Betty had slept through decades of marriage, and shot himself.

"They were a distinguished couple," Betty says, as she eats the last of a blueberry muffin. "Your grandparents really were."

My mother's bed has been moved against the wall. She is already receding from the room. Life is flowing on, but she does not stir her fingers into movement. Betty talks at length of my grandparents, Emily and John. "Every fourth Sunday at Rogers' Grove, the services were in Czech. I asked Gene who was that white-haired man playing the organ so beautifully, and the sun was shining on his beautiful white hair and the pump organ. And Gene said, 'Oh, that's Uncle John.'"

For years, I did not know that my grandfather had played the organ and wasn't just the farmer who plowed and planted and had migraine headaches that my grandmother would doctor by placing wet grape leaves over his eyes as he lay in the hayloft. And, so, he was a complex man, the one I lived with when I was 4 and 5, and where a father's face would be, his is. "He was wasted," my mother always said. "In those days, being a farmer was so hard. He had to haul water and cut trees for the woodstove, plow with workhorses, muck out the stalls."

I see my grandfather in my mother's wedding video. In his early 60s, his shape is that of a younger man, and the long sleeves of his white shirt are cuffed around the elbows. "He was so musical," Mother said. Yet, he milked cows, fed them, hauled the cans, separated the cream from the buttermilk. When I was 4, I followed him everywhere. I was his shadow.

"And Eugene pointed your grandmother out," Betty went on. *"That's Aunt Emma."*

My grandmother Emily, I've missed. She took me in at age 3 and mothered me after my father's death. My first memories are of her. Her cold hands washing mine, soaping each finger one at a time. She had an orange-strawberry birthmark on her shoulder blade and a split earlobe. They happened at birth, the mark and the split earlobe; she thought both were so ugly. Her standards of excellence were strict. When she was young, she could hardly pin up her black hair into the coils and buns of the time. So kinky, it wanted to escape every comb. There was wilderness and seduction in her face as a girl. When old, she brushed her hair out of its braids before she went to sleep. Her long white hair fell like a kinky, grizzled shawl to her waist. "I have the hair of a colored woman," she'd say. I'd tell her how beautiful it was. It was only after she was long dead that I learned she liked to dance, but my grandfather John didn't dance, so there was no dancing in her life. Long after her death, I learned that her own father, a scholar as well as a farmer who had seen Lincoln's funeral train, liked quiet to read in, and, hearing her practice the piano, would stop and say, "Noise, noise. Stop all that noise!" All her life, people had changed her name, Emily, to Emma, which she hated. Aunt Emma, they called her. Never Emily. Emily, not Emma, regretted that she hadn't been allowed to go to high school. "What I would have given to go to college," she always said. Her mother felt she would be less marriageable if she were educated, and there had been a measles outbreak at school–the one room for eight grades–and her mother feared Emily's face might be scarred. A lovely black-haired, blue-eyed girl whom a missionary fell in love with. He asked her to marry him. But she'd already begun seeing my grandfather and didn't want to hurt him. Yet, she herself wished to become a missionary. Florence, who adored her father, wondered if her mother would have been happier married to the missionary. Beautiful Emily, worked almost to death, her back bent with a dowager's hump from stooping in the fields and garden. Emily, with her eight grades of education, insisted that her daughters, as well as her sons, attend college; for the time, an extraordinary stance. All her children graduated, three with post-graduate degrees. The farm couple sent into the world a minister, a university professor, and two teachers. Yet, hers was a life spent denying the self. In the beginning, it was foisted on her–no practicing piano, no dancing, no high school–and, later, she internalized the denying. When she served chicken, she ate only the neck, that piece I've never seen baked anywhere else. Her suppers always consisted of rye bread and instant coffee. She liked fat and the ends of meat that others would not touch. In the end, it pleased her to deny herself. A secret pleasure. She died of stomach cancer.

"And, you know, your mother lived in our farmhouse before Gene was born. She lived there during the week so she could walk with Francis the mile and a half to country school," Betty says, wiping her mouth with a napkin.

My mother draws another harsh breath. Is Florence hearing Betty's voice or has she gone further away?

Yes, she had stayed in the Skalsky house as a child and hated it. Child-rearing practices were different then. Children did as they were told. My grandfather's sister, Lydia, had married Frank Skalsky, and their firstborn son, Francis, was for a long time an only child. When Francis reached age 6, he was ready for first grade at Jappa Country School. Great-aunt Lydia worried about Francis walking the dirt roads alone, and it was decided that Florence would be the one to walk with him to and from school. During the week, she would live with the Skalskys. Girl behind the door. The middle child, the overlooked one, she could be spared.

While Betty talks, I am imagining my mother, with her charge, beginning the dirt road mile to country school. She's holding Francis's hand. Nothing stops the wind; not the long underwear under her gray dress or the clunky boots. Her teeth chatter and she's hoping the school's potbelly stove will be stoked; hot, hotter. How would it be to stand in front of the room, to tell the first-grade readers to come forward to recite? While the fourth-grade readers study their figures, the next group of students prepares to be called. Someday, she'll teach. She does not want to go back to the Skalskys, to eat supper and help with the dishes, to study, and then go to bed in the shivering upstairs.

Snow is falling hard now, with wind behind it.

Abide With Me

Chaplain Barbara enters the room, a tall, handsome woman, soft-spoken and blonde. The Hospice pastor, for those who request prayer, wears beige-colored slacks and a matching jacket. The ability to soothe rather than excite must be a requirement for Hospice employment. The nervous whirling dervishes need not apply.

"I'm surprised to see your mother like this," she says, studying the comatose woman on the bed. "I visited her last week and she was sitting up. She told me that both her parents were musical."

Between last week and today, Florence had stopped breathing. An ambulance was called on Monday night and my brother followed it to Mercy Hospital. "Once she got there, her breathing kicked back in," Joel said. That night, he had called me in New York City and my middle brother in Texas. "I'm here at ground zero with Mom. Hospice has been brought in. If she stops breathing again, they won't be calling an ambulance. That's it. Game over." On Tuesday, I spoke with her. "Stephanie, I don't think I'll live much longer. Last night they woke me from my sleep and took me to the hotel. Remember–only what's done for God will count."

That was the last time she said my name.

"Florence, how are you?" the chaplain asks. "I remember you telling me you loved to play the piano and sing."

To be musical. It was what she wanted most from me. I never thought about pleasing my mother once I became a town girl. "Do it to please me. I've done enough for you," she would say. And so she had. Since elementary school, I'd played the piano badly, but once my mother bought an organ, it was the organ she insisted I learn. She herself loved to play. I look at her big hands and envision them on the keyboard. All roads in my mother's life led to church, except for those that carried her dancing.

Music. Her most prized possession was the organ. After Florence divorced Al, we moved from the apartment to a rental house, which my brother jokingly called a Cracker Jack box. The dwelling had one official bedroom. Brett slept upstairs in the attic, where the slanted ceiling was too low for him to stand upright. Florence made her bedroom on the unheated porch, and I got the bedroom, which was no prize, and so cramped I could barely fit between the bed and the dresser. My bed, which was covered by a shabby red spread, is where I studied for tests. There I read *Andersonville*, the opus about the Confederate prisoner-of-war camp. There I read *In Cold Blood*. I read of Nancy Clutter's last hours, tied to her bed in her pajamas, listening while the two drifters murdered her family. I ate Licorice Nibs as Nancy bled. The ex-convicts had chosen the Clutter farmhouse for its look of prosperity, believing the rumor that Herb Clutter kept big money in his safe. I knew no one would rob the Cracker Jack box, because there weren't even any closets, except for one in the bathroom where we all kept our clothes.

The beautiful organ Florence had bought almost filled the thimble-sized living room. I took organ lessons from a girl two years older than me. On Sundays, she played at a little country church, Jordan's Grove Baptist, about three miles north of Central City. After she graduated from high school and went to college, the choir director asked me to take over as organist. I, who hardly practiced, who balked at anything that didn't come easily. A poor choice, indeed.

Chaplain Barbara leans over Florence, speaking softly but slowly into the stone that is my mother's ear. Perhaps Hospice is right; now that the brain has disconnected her vision, her hearing has sharpened. My brother tells me later that he thinks she hears nothing. Florence is wearing a blue-flowered hospital gown today. Since they've begun turning her every four hours and putting an adult diaper on her, she's worn the hospital gown.

"Florence, it's Chaplain Barbara," she says. "I'm here to pray with you. Joel and Stephanie are here." Joel carries in a chair from the breakfast nook so the pastor can sit next to Florence. We arrange the others in a semi-circle, facing my mother.

How beautiful her breathing is, the rise and fall of her chest, no matter how machine-like. The breath of life is keeping her body warm. Chaplain Barbara presses my mother's hand, with its putty-colored puce fingernails. She opens the prayer book and finds scripture, while, a world away outside the windowpane, the sun blazes. It's a cloudless, sapphire-blue summer day. There's a hard business going on in this room with white walls, a room without charm. No real air and light here, no stickiness of green fields. After the Bible verses, the chaplain reads a sermonette about a heavenly homecoming, meant to comfort the sufferer.

Home. I am thinking of my grandmother Emily's long death. The stomach cancer had hollowed her as she lay in Mercy Hospital, with a private round-the-clock nurse in her room, who fell in love with my gentle grandmother. Emily endured gut pain that even morphine couldn't control. "High wall, high wall," she kept crying out. The wall that she had to climb in order to die. "Let me go home," she kept saying. My mother felt sure it was her desire to be taken home to the Lord, but I suspect it was her farm she was begging for. The four stories, from cellar to attic, of the farmhouse; the bleeding-heart flowers throwing themselves over the orchard fence; the mash of leaves in the water trough. Chaplain Barbara is talking about the welcoming Lord. I think of the welcoming barn and smell hay, hear the cows lowing, milk pinging into the bucket, cream floating to the top of the bucket along with yellow buttermilk. Bridge to the sacred.

"Is there a hymn your mother might like to hear?" the Chaplain asks.

"Abide With Me," Joel suggests.

The chaplain nods, and then a rich soprano voice bubbles out of this tall blonde's mouth. *Abide with me, fast falls the eventide*, she sings, trying to reach, and ease, the woman on the bed. I can hardly see for the tears streaming down my face, making my nose run. Her voice is lush as the summer afternoon. The song is for us, I think, but I'm not sure.

⁂

"Abide With Me" surely was one of the simple songs I had played at Jordan's Grove, where you could smell the muskiness and the pull-rope of the bell. From the organist's bench, I could view the framed portraits of the past ministers as they peered into the pews. A toy of a church for its handful of worshippers. I would practice the songs with the choir director on Wednesdays after school, and since I was 16 going on 17, Florence let me use the Rambler to drive the three miles to the country church. A mistake of trust on her part. I don't think she realized how impulsive and oblivious of danger her daughter was.

"I was never so proud of you as when you played the organ at that little church," Florence said repeatedly.

I must have been the worst organist ever to grace a bench. Fear gripped me as I began a hymn; I closed my eyes to keep time, to not strike a wrong note. But the seat I really should never have sat on was the driver's seat.

Wednesday, and I'd made a right turn off the two-lane highway. The speedometer registered 65 mph and already the Rambler had torn up the gravel road, the dashboard blasting Grace Slick singing "White Rabbit." I stepped on the gas. The speedometer read 70, then 75. *I'm traveling fast. Everything gets prettier with speed.* The alfalfa and corn rushed by. I pressed the accelerator. Flying fast, faster, the Rambler galloped, ready to leap into the sky. The car flew up the incline near Darnell Lindley's farm, gravel churning on either side. When the Rambler crested the hill, I saw a stalled pickup in the middle of the road. High wooden sides, the bed overflowing with shelled corn, no blinker lights flashed out of the dusted-over back taillights. No room to get around the truck, and the flying Rambler was going so fast. The truck had waited for me. I hit the brakes and turned the wheel, aiming for the ditch. The car fishtailed, hitting the truck. *This is it.* No seat belt. No fear. Nothing. In the field, a pond of cow run-off, its muddy water floated lily pads of dung.

My forehead scraped over the dashboard. I am here; then, instantly, I'm gone.

Someone going by called the sheriff. The farmer with the stalled truck turned out to be Mr. Smith. He had the bad luck to be standing in front of his vehicle with the hood up. When the back of the Rambler hit his bumper, his truck ran him over. The ambulances came and we were rushed to St. Luke's Hospital in Cedar Rapids.

This accident began my *time of troubles.* I had hurt someone by driving too fast; I'd broken Farmer Smith's hips and he would never farm again. My license would soon be suspended. The highway patrol measured the skid marks and claimed I was going 90 mph.

For two days, I drifted in and out of consciousness. When I finally came to, my boyfriend, Bill Boyle, a dark-eyed, half Cherokee long-hair, sat beside the bed. Later, my mother complained that his pants were too tight to be in a hospital room. A storyteller in the oral tradition of indigenous people, he knew everything about Central City residents, everyone's secrets, and stayed on the lookout for more gossip. He was the first to tell the town that Mary Carley and Chris Sauer had hit the Santa Fe Northwestern train; the first to let it be known that when Kenny Akers came home from walking point in Vietnam, he had molested the papergirl, whose mother decided to let it go. When Doug Hills got discharged from the Marine Corps with a steel plate in his head, he swallowed whole bottles of aspirin with his beer. In Bill's view, Doug Hills, who liked women better than anyone he'd ever met, had been run off the road on his motorcycle by a jealous man. Six women cried at Doug's funeral, and two of them were wearing maternity clothes. Then there was Frank Bruce, who attempted suicide when the big Indian chick, Roxanne, dumped him.

"You're real lucky to be alive," Bill said, pushing his hair back from his forehead.

A woman walked into the room. Maybe she was lost. A farm woman, with nicely set brown hair and her lipstick–the orange of Sloppy Joe barbecue–in the middle of her mouth. She held her denim chore-coat closed with a callused hand. "I'm Mrs. Smith," she said, in a kindly voice. "I just came to tell you…." Her voice broke off as her eyes reddened and she came closer to lean over me, tears seeping from her like trough water. "It was an accident," she said, stroking my hand. "We don't blame you. It was an accident. We believe that, and we're praying for you. Like we're praying for Dad." I wondered if *Dad* was her father or her husband.

I bit my lip and wanted to giggle. Like in church choir when everyone was silent.

Mrs. Smith stared at me.

"I'm sorry!" I said. "I'm so sorry!" I don't know why I felt like laughing.

I learned that Farmer Smith was a deacon and a Farm Bureau treasurer; he had two sons, two daughters, eight grandchildren, and one great-granddaughter. That's not how I remembered him. I saw an older man, covered with dust like an oil can in the DX, his shadowy figure tinkering in the gold pollen that sifted from the truck's bed. I'd wanted to go fast, to leave the earth and Iowa behind. I'd decided to fly.

Farmer Smith was the penance that I would have to pay.

⁂

Later, I had a court date in the little white building where traffic violations were adjudicated. An officer from the highway patrol was there to testify about the skid marks he had measured. I was charged with FAILURE TO HAVE VEHICLE UNDER CONTROL. The estimated speed of my mother's blue Rambler was 90 mph. An unsafe speed, especially on a gravel road. My mother sat beside me in a folding chair. I was totally in the wrong, yet, Florence, who was quick to find fault with me at home, tried to stand up for my driving abilities to the highway patrol officer. The Traffic Court judge ordered my license suspended for six months. I would never renew it, never drive again, nor have the slightest desire to sit behind the wheel of a car.

Jordan's Grove would have to find a new organist. I would miss Sunday mornings; the rope, like a hay pulley, ringing the bell. Most of the truly faithful were lying under stones in the church graveyard with goldenrods in their throats. Jordan's Grove. That's where I played the hymns I didn't practice, that's where I dreamed about the faraway places I would visit, and fidgeted with the terrible impatience to get to where the streets teemed with people. Where I would come over the hill and press down on the accelerator. Now I've been to those faraway places, and have found that nothing compares to the green summers of Iowa.

Corn Wind

I wonder if Florence wouldn't want music to fill the white-walled room; so airless, devoid of mood. Not the type of room you want to leave life in. Joel surprises me; he's found a CD player and borrowed it, along with two Old Favorite Hymn compilations.

"Later, kiddo," he says. Then he talks to our mother before leaving. "Brett is on the way. He'll be here tomorrow morning."

Brett, who was here in Iowa three weeks earlier, is flying back. I take out Florence's Bible, her Anchor House devotionals, the CD of hymns. I gather up her photograph album. These are the weapons with which to confront death. I've been taught all my life that there are no atheists in the foxholes.

I put the CD of hymns in the player and "Jesus Loves Me," sung in a stark, almost hillbilly, twang, rises from the speakers. A pure soprano voice. Upon seeing the song title, I dismissed it as the one sing-songed by children. It fills the room, pushes back the whiteness, the doorless toilet, the desk with my mother's folded glasses, and her loafers with nylon anklets balled inside. I watch Florence's face carefully. She would like *this* song; the simplicity and childlike quality of the rendition might still speak to her melting mind. Proud of her Buresh family, which had struggled out of Bohemia with five sons, making their way to Iowa in the midst of a raging American Civil War. How uninviting and futureless Europe must have been for my ancestors to have taken their lives in their hands and left. They shunned Catholics. They would not allow crosses in their houses of worship. The Catholic priests had come to persecute the Protestants, holding the crosses before them, the torches right behind. These were the years that Bibles were hidden in cow pies and dung. *Jesus Loves Me, This I Know.* A man who lived two thousand years ago in Galilee, a long-haired, dusty-footed wanderer, loves you. Does the brain cutting off communication with the eyes love Jesus? Is it our better selves that aspire to goodness and love? I remember, above my six-year-old bed, a card of blue felt cradling the head of Christ, his flowing hair and a glowing cross. He watches over me; no harm will come from the night, with its dark places with no eyes.

I read the Lord is my Shepherd psalm. I read it over and over aloud. Death feels stronger than these beautiful metaphors. I open the photograph albums and start to tell Florence what I see in these captured snapshots. I watch the impossible. My little pony of a mother is dying. My childhood is dying too. I picture the farmhouse as it was then; the outbuildings, the horse pasture, the orchard. This is *home,* where Florence will return, where I too will return. I am riding my bicycle down Zahradnik's Hill. I see the field girl Florence, in her cotton dress and wide-brimmed hat, her hair blowing in the corn wind. Inside she feels clumsy as a bumpkin, but how fresh and dewy she appears on the outside. I tell my mother how I see her in the field at the beginning of her life. How beautiful she is in the corn wind. The next hymn is "Rock of Ages" and then "A Mighty Fortress."

Her machine-breathing continues. I stroke her hand. Kissing her forehead again, I try to say the right things.

Mother, of rural teacher certification and outhouses, of soft cistern rainwater for hair and hard water for drinking; Mother, who showed me how to crack an egg and run my finger inside the shell to get all of the egg white and birth yolk, the gift of another species' young. Mother, of county exams; you'll take them and be able to teach one-room school; shy country bumpkin is how you describe yourself, too shy to make friends in the city high school, where you sit at lunch, eating your bread and molasses alone. Mother, of the flat irons, the two-burner stove, the cold of your first teaching job, 40 dollars a month, then a new job that paid 5 dollars more a month; Tracy, Iowa; then Walnut. Mother, eating half a meatloaf sandwich for lunch for a nickel, not wanting to spend a dime on the whole sandwich. Mother, who gave cracked boards names that you and your brother would drag through the orchard, through a childhood of broken dishes and corncrib slats. Mother, of winters when the water in the slough froze; sharing one pair of rusty ice skates with your brother, taking turns, one watching while the other skated, and when it was the shy girl's turn, you fell and hit your head so hard on the ice, you saw stars. Florence, the last living child of the family you were born into. It feels like the farmhouse is on fire and all the walls are falling in–horehounds, the wicker carriage, plum trees.

⁂

Brett calls to tell us when he will arrive. He asks me to phone Aunt Mary Elizabeth in Dallas, our uncle Fred's widow. A native of Helena, Montana, she had met Uncle Fred during WWII, or *The War,* as that generation refers to the great cataclysm. A fledgling pilot, he had trained at the Army Air Base in Helena before shipping out overseas. The Air Corp was the Army's branch of aviation. The Air Force was not in existence yet. He had met her at a youth group dance and fallen in love with her bronze-red ringlets and exquisite manners. Eighteen then, the Montana girl who married my uncle seemed bred to the role of minister's wife: never raising her voice, expecting "pardon me" and "excuse my reach" from her children at the table. It was too difficult for the mouths of children to say *Aunt Mary Elizabeth*, so she was dubbed *Aunt Penny.*

I envision Grandmother's living room, where Uncle Fred and Aunt Penny would arrive for a Sunday afternoon visit. The farmhouse would settle into that peaceful afternoon lull, the day of rest, coffee percolating and kolaches warming in the oven. Apricot, prune, strawberry, cherry, cottage cheese kolaches. The summer orchard would fill the house with the aroma of ripening apples, the breeze drifting through the window screens. I was almost 4 years old, and didn't know yet that my father had died forever. Grandfather relaxed on the cattail davenport, its brown nap dense like that of the ditch reeds. Uncle Fred was tall and strong, a laughing man. He picked me up and hoisted me on his shoulders, the whole world shifting. The floor, with its cabbage rose carpet so far down and the shoulders bouncing me ever higher. I was breathless with fright, but somehow knew I was safe.

Aunt Penny's hair glowed a chestnut red, red and bronze, twin colors woven together the deeper I peered. We called her *Aunt Penny*, since the curls of her hair were pennies and freckles. On her right hand, she wore a ring with a large amber stone, which dazzled as if all the beauty of childhood had been captured inside. Uncle Fred and Aunt Penny lived with their three children in a manse in Vinton, Iowa, a house that the church provided to its minister. In the manse, there were bits of loveliness: ruby glasses, fruits in a glass bowl, grapes that never aged, apples with their ripeness painted on, pears in their blush. In the stillness of the manse, the smell of trees drifted.

Now I key in the number and my aunt answers the phone. In her 80s, her mind seems clear and crisp, her diction precise, her voice musical. Just as I remember it.

"How are you?" I ask. It has been over a year since Uncle Fred died.

"Your uncle was a good man and gave me a beautiful life. I miss him, and sometimes think he's just gone on a mission and will be coming back. That, after a marriage of sixty years."

Uncle Fred, a retired minister, took a computer class when he was 87 and entered the Internet age. But Mom, although attracted to the magic of finding a health article in seconds and printing it out, would say "Kabash! I've had to learn enough in my life." She called CDs *circles.* Brett was always mailing her *circles* with photos of his children, of graduation and school plays; circles that stayed in their envelopes. When she saw me using the mouse on my laptop, she asked if I was typing in sentences or boxes.

The room pauses as Florence draws a harsh breath.

"Is your mother living her last days?" my aunt asks.

I break down in tears, almost unable to say the one word. "Yes."

"Your mother was our hero. Fred and I admired and loved her. She had many disappointments in her life. To lose a fiancé in the war. To grieve for a young husband and raise three children alone. To learn Braille in order to take a teaching job. To marry again and have her husband treat her unkindly. All this, and yet, she carried on. She had a sense of humor. So much tickled her."

"Aunt Penny, would you like me to hold the phone to her ear so you can talk to her?"

"Yes, Stephy, I would like that."

We address each other with the nicknames of long ago. I stretch the cord to Florence's phone, devised for the hard of hearing, with amplification that could crack open stones. I can easily hear my aunt's clear voice burbling like creek water into her ears. Words of love, words of comfort.

I ponder the word *tickled* for the rest of the night. I picture Florence in her black pedal-pushers and zebra blouse, sitting in the farmhouse kitchen, laughing at some witticism. Dinner has just finished and her two brothers are still at the table. Both of my uncles had a dry wit, and Florence laughed so hard, she slapped her leg, almost choking. I laugh and hit my leg like that when something truly amuses me.

⁂

I never saw my mother cry until the last year of her life. It was as astonishing as water springing from rock. Ten months ago, in September, when I visited for two weeks, she cried. Joel was flying to Thailand and would be traveling to Laos and Vietnam. "He's going to China," she said, unable to think of the names of those blurred Southeast Asian countries. Mother felt sure she would never see him again, and the tears trickled down her face. I knew then that this was not the Florence I'd known most of my life. "Mom, Mom," I said, putting my arm around her. "Yes, you'll see him again. Yes, you will." And she did see him again.

⁂

There are more fireflies in the Iowa night than anywhere else in the country. I part the blinds over the bed in the Memory Care Unit room where I sleep. The lights are off. Everywhere in the parking lot, the glowing lanterns dart and spark. Will my mother live through the night? Tell me, fireflies.

In the days I've sat beside Florence's bed, I've heard the stories of other women; the nurses and aides tell me how their mothers and grandmothers passed. Diabetes and amputations, heart attacks during the Super Bowl, ovarian cancer. Passing. Homegoing. The rite like no other. Angie, the African-American nurse, tells me, "Your mother is afraid to go home."

"Me a good Christian" is one of the last four sentences she spoke. Could the nearness of death have set free the frightened girl, trudging to a one-room school under the gray sky; released the adult woman in the grip of menopause nightmares, where snakes slithered under her bed? Those farmhouse nights when I was 10 or 11 and would wake hearing the moaning coming from my mother's frozen room. In winter, her windows were always open. Often, she would scream in her sleep. Now my mother's wailing is silenced by morphine, not by the Anchor Houses and Logs of the Good Ship Grace; not by the psalms I read to her.

Tonight, the nurse from West Virginia who calls herself *Squirrel* brought my mother's morphine around dinnertime. Red-haired, a smoker, her deep voice full of laughter, she insisted I have something to eat from the kitchen. I made my way to the dining hall, where residents suffering from Alzheimer's ate the food they no longer remembered the names of. The vats bubbled along. A turkey paste soup. Forlorn green beans wanting to go back into their cans. Vanilla pudding mixed with Dole's fruit cocktail. Yellow cake frosted hot pink. I took a tray back to my mother's room and tried to eat, but could not. I waited until the dining room closed and then went to the kitchen and emptied the soup and green beans into the garbage and washed the dishes. This is the food my mother ate during the last year.

* *

The food I ate in those first months after the shooting had to be semi-liquid. The days of my convalescence, in Vinton, began early. Aunt Patsy and Uncle Douglas got up shortly after dawn to ready themselves for the dental office. I was awake, drifting in sleeplessness. My grandmother and I were alone in the house on Country Club Drive all day. It was the land of quiet, and what little noise we made, the willow carpet absorbed. Mornings, I went through the house; I stared out each of the windows and saw different futures in them. In one future I would never leave the house, I would bury myself in closets, and in another I'd go to college and become a writer; in yet another I would marry Michael (or some unknown) and bear his child; in yet another I would once again stand beside the highway with my thumb out.

I liked the feel of the thick green carpet in the sunken living room. The entire back living room wall was a window that faced the frozen Meadowview Country Club. With my eyes I wandered the golf course, its pond with stiffened cattails and rushes that stuck up through the ice; I joined the nuthatches and woodpeckers, the starlings, the hardy ones that stayed for the winter and circled the miniature slough. Afternoons, it was quiet as a dead bird in the house, the quiet of pausing, knowing little would happen that did not happen yesterday; it was the quiet of my grandmother's waiting. I could enter her loneliness now that most of her generation had gone into the silence. Yet, she was still here, in the modern avocado-green kitchen with the island enamel stove and the self-defrosting refrigerator. I watched her stir the chicken soup, homemade noodles cut so thin I'd be able to suck them through my teeth. Uncle Douglas said he would soon cut the wires, as scraping the enamel off my teeth seemed all that the Duke University dentists had managed to do, failing to move my jaw into alignment. In my new life, I would hate to chew; it would be a thirst that I needed forever to quench. In the afternoon's doldrums I locked myself in my aunt and uncle's master bathroom. I hoisted myself up and hunched between the *his* and *her* sinks, holding a hand mirror and comparing in the larger mirror my left side to my right side.

I loved my grandmother effortlessly, she who let me hold her hands, who let me kiss her. We kept company; she was my ragdoll, who let me sit next to her with my arm around her. Her cold hands soothed me, and she didn't mind that I traced their veins, the rivers running under the freckled skin, so bruise-blue they were almost black. I traced the marks the cooking knife left in her fingers, the nicks and cuts. At 4 p.m., *Green Acres* came on, then *Gomer Pyle*, and my grandmother and I would watch; we would listen to the canned laughter and idiocies. I'd regressed to an earlier age, no longer 18, more like 11.

When I swallowed the liquid Demerol, the dirty waves of heat struck, washing over me, ebbing then flowing, pulsating in my eyelids and temples, the blood vessels in my brain constricting, and red anger, like two predator animals, rushed through the rest of me. I wanted to hit the walls, tear the carpet, and pick my skin off. My grandmother clutched me, her whole body cold as her hands. Bent from stooping in the field, from planting and weeding, so bowed she couldn't straighten her back, she held me together. Her bones hugged me, her skeleton comforted. Once, my mother came to Vinton to spend the weekend and the Demerol shook me with its sticky, furious heat, and I cried and tried to sit in her lap. Her face drained away into the two lines on either side of her mouth. She would not hold me; she had turned to ice. "You ruined your own life. Don't blame me. No one told you to carry yourself to North Carolina." She needed someone to comfort *her*, some lap to climb into.

Nights, the February moon shone in the window along with the icicled streetlights. Those first winter months when I was only weeks out of the hospital, when I slept in Aunt Patsy and Uncle Douglas's guest room, were nights of torture. The warm bed, a rack. Nights were the most terrible because you had to go to bed, you had to try and sleep on a double bed with sheets and blankets that felt like flames. The intense burning pain in my hand worsened. The lightning strikes began. For sleep I'd been prescribed liquid Thorazine that my uncle drew up in an eyedropper and mixed with orange juice. Hours dragged by before the Thorazine kicked in and sleep came. Nothing could douse the dry brush wildfire of damaged nerves, misfiring from outer space. Random sunspots. The fire smoldered in my fingers, and by flexing them open with my other hand, I could release some of the sparks. More tossing, more turning. When I could no longer bear it, I got up and went to the window. I liked looking at the snowdrifts. I knuckled myself against the glass; I pressed my burning arm into the frost. I wanted to lie down in the snow; I could sleep on the ice. How I hated the guest room, with the radiators pumping out their monotonous low heat. I wanted a bed in the snow.

My college acceptance came from a new state university in southwestern Minnesota. I would enroll in March for the spring quarter, with Rehabilitation of Iowa paying my tuition. It was my last chance, Florence warned me.

Michael wrote letters, sometimes two a day, and always two on Monday, because Sunday's letter arrived with it. This was the year Bernardine Dohrn's Wanted Poster stared down from the heights of the post office bulletin board, the post office with its odor of stalled mail, each slotted box with its combination a mystery, the post office where my uncle Douglas and I would stop to pick up his dental office checks. These were my outings. The red, white, and blue flag that waved outside no longer meant the Memorial Day Parade and marching as a pom-pom girl. The flag now rankled; the flag meant protests and draft card burnings. The flag meant Bernardine Rae Dohrn. WANTED BY THE FBI. FOR INTERSTATE FLIGHT–MOB ACTION; RIOT; CONSPIRACY. Her height, 5'5"; her weight, 125 pounds. Hair: Dark Brown. I studied the expression on her face–not frightened or vacant but self-possessed. The Weatherman high priestess, said to be a brainiac, looked like a model. Her combat boots held her ensemble together, the black jeans tucked into her boot tops, the leather jacket unzipped and the collar open at her neck, the sleeves a little too long, as if the jacket belonged to a man. Except for her face and its pale skin like a lily or altar cloth, everything about her was dark, to match the curtains of her hair.

Letters from Michael kept arriving. In one, he told me that Charlie, no longer a long-hair, was bragging about the shooting in the Raleigh bars. The day would come (in a year) when a letter arrived from the District Attorney of Wake County, North Carolina, inquiring whether or not I wanted to press charges against Charles Dunham for Reckless Endangerment, his Depraved Indifference to Human Life. I declined to. Prison time for Charlie would not return what had been taken. Fifteen years later, Charlie, who'd graduated from college and worked as a computer programmer at IBM, who'd married Janet and had children, was found dead. Besides owning his suburban home, he kept a trailer in the woods where he often went to relax. He had been missing for two days when his family looked for him at the trailer. They found him lying dead between tanks partially filled with nitrous oxide. He'd overdosed on laughing gas.

Florence Becomes a Firefly

The morning of June 29th dawns cloudless, with a blue sky. It will be another hot day. As soon as I wake, I run down the hall. Is she still breathing? Florence hasn't moved, although last night they rolled her onto her side to change her sheet and adult Pampers. I want to tell her that only for four days was she humbled in this way. The body has finished digesting and evacuating. Hands at her sides, she lies in the hospital bed, chest rising, expelling her rough breaths. Her feet are purple; the mottling is taking place. I kiss her forehead again and again, saying *Mom, Mom.* I run back down the hall to shower, happy that she's still warm. I understand now why some relatives of those in vegetative comas do not want their loved ones to be let go; they applaud the heroic hopeless measures. Just to feel the blood's warmth, to be near the animal presence, is enough. Life is short. Death lasts forever.

I return to Florence's room, move the tape player close, prepare the religious hymn CD. The aide, Ashley, comes in with a plastic bucket filled with fingernail polishes and removers. She is in her twenties, a single mother; her dishwater blonde hair, tied back from her chubby face, allows her greasy blue eyes an unobstructed view. Her eyes, I've noticed before, the voyeur's. "Florence," she says to my prone mother, who is making a snoring sound. "Would you like me to polish your nails?" My mother's mouth is slightly agape.

I ask her to remove the mauve from Florence's fingernails and then trim her toenails. I've noticed that her big toenail is jagged. Otherwise, her feet do not look 98 years old; they are pliable and pink, the nails soft. Last year for her birthday, I had bought her a manicure set.

"Sure," Ashley says, sitting on the bed and placing my mother's hand in her lap.

A picture rises in my mind, or maybe my hands picture helping my grandmother Emily cut her toenails. "Don't," she told me. "They're so ugly." We were in the farmhouse kitchen. She was sitting in a wooden straight-backed chair, wearing her white work dress printed with tiny yellow flowers. She'd taken off her brown stockings and her feet were bare. I'd never seen her in pants. At 10 years old, I sat on the floor with the clippers. If I turned, I could see the orchard's apple trees through the living room window's lace curtains. The hay balers had left the fields and the stillness filled with the late cooing of the mourning dove. My grandmother listened too, and we stayed quiet together. We were the old woman and girl they had forgotten.

Emily looked out over the gulf that separated her from her feet; a lifetime of work in the garden, planting and weeding; of laundry days, using scrub board, then ringer washer; another lifetime of hanging the wash to line-dry, winters in the cellar and summers outside to capture the breeze in clean sheets, of ironing, sprinkling clothes with rainwater, heating flat irons scoured first with cedar boughs, then heaving them across the endless white tablecloths and laced mutton-leg sleeves. The easier tasks of bread-making, noodle-making, jam, jelly, mushrooming, baking; all that work etched on her thin body, whittled away her flesh, stiffened her joints. Yet, after raising children and grandchildren, she was still able to work harder than I.

But she couldn't reach her feet to cut her toenails. "You'll hurt your hands," she warned. I was already bent to the task and fascinated by the foreign country of her feet. The acorn shapes of her bunions from badly fitting leather boots; the big toe and little toe were seeded with corns, like field kernels, only harder. And the nails themselves tough as gravel, thickened, each a miniature dowager's hump. I fit them between the clipper blades and they crumbled away. This I could easily do for my grandmother. The late afternoon sun shone in the farmhouse windows, the west-facing kitchen. A mistake, my mother had always said, the kitchen never to receive the strong morning light to warm a winter hearth, yet, in summer, flooded with the sun's glare. I adored my grandmother. A love pure as well water. A love not muddied with anger like the love between a mother and daughter. Afterwards, she thanked me.

"My feet are so ugly," she repeated with a laugh.

"Nothing about you is ugly," I told her.

"I always wanted to learn," she said, looking into the sun. "Now it's too late."

Even in the worst of my late teen years of bad living, of drugging and throwing money away; even when my college friends skipped and dropped classes and took incompletes, trying for their degrees with the least amount of effort, I loved the classes, the lectures, the effort. I never forgot my grandmother's desire. A gifted, intelligent woman fated to be a farmer's wife, a workhorse. What was it like for Emily to covet her brother's college studies? To climb the stairs in summer when no one was bothering the books, to enter his room and kneel by the desk and reach for them? In her hands, a book, the smooth skin of the cover, so forbidden, so different from the wooden spoon, the knife, the scrub board, the rag, the hoe, the harness, the grist stone. The opening of a book, Latin, to touch the words, to taste them whispered in her mouth. Her mother's voice coming after her: "Go fetch the clothes from the line."

And, so, she sent her own daughters to college.

⁂

Florence. Emily's second daughter, her third child, the last living child, has only hours left. The skin on Florence's face that she's always taken care of seems to smooth itself of wrinkles, as if the morphine has waved its wand, wiping all expression and emotion from it. Ashley's glistening eyes match the pools of polish remover in which she douses a cotton ball. I sense her excitement; she's anxious not to miss out on anything, and she keeps popping in and out of the room, apparently wanting to be here to see my mother die.

I think of Aunt Penny's valiant phone call, which had yielded no response from my mother, no recognition of her sister-in-law's voice. Today, the same. Nothing is getting into *Florence.* I watch her face closely. Not a twitch, not a blink. A Botox mask. Those first two days when she was wailing, some sensory impressions still made their way in, especially when the gentle nurse, Diana, said her name. *Florence.* I hear her name again and again. I've never liked the name Florence; unpretty and old-fashioned. Clunky, like a Rambler. Now I find it beautiful. Everything about my mother I rebelled against; the religion, the criticism, her name, her face, her car, her profession, her music, her scarves, her raincoats, her hand-washing, her financial responsibility, her scrimping and saving. Whatever stance she took, I stood against it. It didn't matter what I preferred, only that it be the opposite of my mother's preference. *Florence.* I say *Florence* aloud. *Florence Ruth.* A pretty name. I never knew that until today.

On that second day, she was still wailing, but during a moment when she was more lucid, her last words to me were, "Thank you, girl." She could feel me rubbing her back and holding her, but she did not know it was her daughter. Had she heard the female voice? *Thank you, girl.*

When Rob calls, I ask him to tell Florence goodbye. He had made four trips to Iowa with me. My mother has always liked him; his bigness, his humility. "He eats so much," she once said. Again I stretch the cord of the extreme-amplification phone. I can hear his voice, his soothing telephone manner. Then I see what almost looks like a blink, an eye trying to open for a moment. Who might she think he is? Her father, her brother, Luther, Philip, or does she recognize him as Rob?

* *

I return to that first time Rob and I took the Greyhound to Iowa, when we believed we'd signed in to the lower class. It was official–we were white trash (self-made, at that). The college- educated were rarely denizens of bus depots, and while we held three advanced degrees between us, we had been unable to translate them into financial success. In Philadelphia, the bus took on more travelers. Anna and Robert, newlyweds, plopped into the seats in front of us. Her abundant flesh smelled of overripe muskmelon and baby powder. Pink glasses perched on her pretty face as she listened to her husband. They'd spent their one-night-long honeymoon at the Star Wars Museum in Philadelphia. "We saw robot droids of Luke Skywalker and Darth Vader." The couple felt as if they'd gone far into the future; they touched the Force and were carrying it back to Pittsburgh. Anna weighed two hundred pounds, while her man was slender, handsome, and so friendly we wondered if he was possibly of low intelligence. "Having my arms and neck covered makes me feel safer," Anna said. Obligingly, her husband nestled his head against her neck and kissed her cheek and ear. She allowed him his kisses, then said, "Hand me the Little Debbie's." He dug into a brown paper grocery bag and found the Little Debbie's fudge bars. Anna and Robert belonged to a bowling team. The Pittsburgher Boosters.

Dusk, the smokestacks of Pittsburgh greeted us, Steel City, USA, now trickling strings of anemic smoke into the iron sky. Goodbye to Anna and Robert, to the Pittsburgher Glee Club. On we jolted into the fading American night, haunted by the buffalo and bumblebee. Florence waited for us in the heartland.

"I can see prairie dogs, and they're wearing collars of fireflies. Can you see them too?" I asked.

Rob nodded. "And do you hear the cricket choirs?"

We both could. Riding a bus across the country, you can see the sadness of our land. The accumulation of junk, the parking lots crowding out the green, the trees and foliage bedraggled, towns either half-abandoned or overcrowded. Who could be sure of its name, what to call the tangling power lines, the strip malls, the plague spreading from town to town. Yet, we held hands; we were happy.

⁂

We arrived in Cedar Rapids. A taxi had to be called, and arrived twenty minutes later, and for 23 dollars we were ferried across cowtown to Village Place. Once inside my mother's apartment, I opened her refrigerator to get ice cubes from the freezer. Every nook and cranny of the freezer was stuffed with Swanson TV dinners, tiny bags of half-eaten beef patties tied with string, and crumbling walnuts, but no ice cube tray.

"Mom, where's your ice cube tray?" I asked. "I'd like some ice."

Florence rolled her eyes. "You people can't have everything you want."

After almost two days on a bus, it was my turn to roll my eyes.

"You people can eat some TV dinners, if you can stand it." My mother explained she was no longer cooking, as she'd forgotten how.

But we couldn't stand it after two days of cellophane food marinated in chemicals. We were ready to vomit. By the next day, my mother liked Rob immensely and couldn't understand his mental illness, why he couldn't work. "He sure can eat," she announced two days later. For the first time in her apartment's life, no leftovers remained behind to be stowed in her Tupperware containers.

⁂

Summer is her favorite season, and today in Iowa, June 29th, it is hot, a heat-wave day, a taste of what is coming. Greenhouse gases trapped, rice no longer able to grow in Texas, cattle being moved into Nebraska, horses abandoned and starving and dying of thirst in the Southwest, aquifers almost depleted, water polluted. This is the world Florence is escaping, although today Iowa looks green, lushly beautiful, even despite climate change. *The funny weather,* she called it. I would talk to her on Sundays, our longest conversation of the week. She often spoke of *funny weather.* The snowstorms falling hard, and by noon, melting. "I don't drive anymore, so it doesn't matter." Born into a world of seasons, she is leaving a world of funny weather.

I think of Florence's hesitation about moving to Village Ridge–the death house. I think of how she feared no longer being trusted to remember her own name. The demon Alzheimer's roamed its halls.

"Mom, you can't take all these lids into your new apartment," my brothers had said. "There's no room."

"These things are my life," she'd cried out in protest at the thought of any of her possessions being discarded, i.e., the thousands of plastic containers, the threadbare towels, the costume jewelry and clip-on earrings. "You people will throw everything away. In my day, children divided up their folks' things." It is a very different day–a disposable one–and nothing is sacred. Her cupboards were still stocked with the foods of my childhood: Jeno's pizza, rock-hard Jiffy biscuit mix, melted Tang and Ovaltine, crumbling *me too!* graham crackers, wax paper.

"Mom, only what's absolutely necessary moves with you," Joel said. "Nothing that isn't mission-imperative."

"Nerts!" she said, stamping her foot. "You people."

My brothers made secret trips to the dumpster, throwing out forty garbage bags of margarine containers, cottage cheese containers, oleo, and yogurt tubs still bearing the indecipherable names of brands that had long disappeared from store shelves. Detritus, things in pieces, remnants. My father's watch. The rose glass candy dish with its lid missing. Screws that fit nowhere, skeleton keys to doors in torn-down houses. In my mother's day, billions fewer people walked the planet's surface; her kind saved everything– they were pleasure-misers in an age where self-abnegation was a virtue. They shopped in grocery stores, not supermarkets. Watermelons meant it was late June, the black-seeded red flesh ripe for sale gone by August's end. Oranges, a Christmas treat. They said *darn*, not *damn*; *number 2*, not *shit*. Florence never threw anything away, and I watched the things of my childhood age in their own way, some becoming relics, like the tin picnic basket that carried its last picnic to the park in her 98th year.

**

And now, in the white-walled room so unlike the farmhouse where she was born and raised, where I was raised, I sit in the chair beside her bed. The indestructible Florence lies in a blue-checked hospital gown, her mouth agape. Are we watching our mother slowly overdose, and isn't it better being lowered gently into the final coma? I think of her panic. "There were times last month when she was wailing, her eyes looking off into some horrible place," Joel had said. There was the time she was getting ready for bed and started to undress in front of us. Brett jumped up. 'Oh, God, Mom! No! Oh, my God!' She was out of her mind. Sure, we've seen her angry and stomping around, but this was *out of her mind*."

Joel stops off in the room, car keys in hand. "Brett is on the way. He'll be here in an hour. I'm going to pick him up from the airport." I wonder if Florence will still be breathing by the time he gets back.

The window drapes are drawn and the white room is filled with June sun. I smell the polish remover. Cutex. A familiar odor. Reassuring. Ashley, who had never learned botany or Latin, who couldn't teach algebra or Beginning Reading like my mother; this Ashley, raised on reality TV and her smoke break, wants to be here for Florence's last breath. All morning she's been running in and out, standing by when Hospice was here, listening.

I wait for her to leave, and then I put the tape of hymns in the CD player. Again the hillbilly voice wafts up, singing "In the Garden," and it is strangely beautiful. I gather up my mother's photograph albums. I start to turn the pages. Maybe it is the Red Cross she loved best, wearing the tailored uniform and poufy bangs and the just-past-the-shoulders hair. A recreation worker–a paid position, she'd always pointed out. In California and Arizona, wearing the nylons so prized during WWII on her shapely Florence Telecky legs. All the attention from returning servicemen. Snapshot after snapshot. Florence with a man in uniform, his arm around the small of her back. There she is at a formal dinner with other Red Cross nurses, and men in uniform on either side of her, a polished wood table with goblets of tinkling water, one of the men, an officer.

Here is a photograph of a long-ago picnic. There's my father and his parents, there's Uncle Morris with the rotund stomach and Aunt Kate with her upswept hair, and this is a

Chicago park. Picnicking, the food you might have eaten at home tastes better. Perhaps the food is happier in the sun. The green everywhere in the black-and-white photograph dazzles. Florence will walk into this day where you can see the willow wands floating. "Mom, it's a beautiful summer day and we're going on a picnic," I say, "and you're wearing your turquoise dress with the white polka dots and strand of white beads." I tell her we're all there. Joel and Brett in their tiny pressed shorts and shirts, their hair parted on the side. I'm in a pink dress that matches the ribbons in my fine hair. There's a breeze. Florence has raised her hand to her bangs to keep them from being mussed. Her Red Cross hair has been trimmed; a married woman and mother of three needs shorter hair. My father is wearing a short-sleeved shirt of opaque material. His black hair is trimmed close to his head; his exceptionally large dark brown eyes are reproduced in the faces of his three children.

In this snapshot, Florence Ruth is sitting on the front steps of the farmhouse; her sister, Vlasta, is standing behind, with her hands resting on Florence's shoulders. The orchard's in full bloom, throwing black-green shadows into the porch windows, as if the two girls had been created from leaf litter.

More Florence. This time she's 12 years old and being confirmed. The photo is formal. The boys in the back row stand awkwardly, sons of the farm in homemade haircuts, their suits with puckered seams. The girls sit on a bench. Florence wears a white puff-sleeved dress, stockings and shoes to match, her ladylike ankles crossed. All the girls' dresses are white. All of them now able to eat the flesh and drink the blood of Christ. They are photographed by the country church in a glade of hickories and oaks. The confirmation class of the dead. My mother is the prettiest of the girls–some are slump-shouldered; others stare at their hands. She holds herself perfectly. Even in old age, she has maintained her good posture. A white rose with ferns and stem is pinned to each girl's upper left shoulder. Reverend Pokorny, whose theological treatises now live under glass in Cedar Rapids' Czech Museum, sits in the front row, a rose in his lapel, one hand inside his jacket like Napoleon, his beard not yet the yellowy-white I remember from childhood, the brown oval surrounding his mouth where the pipe stem stained it. The tobacco smell of his kiss.

From the CD player comes more of the hillbilly twang. *Jesus loves me* surrounds the bed. Florence had a clear soprano voice and loved to sing. "Daddy was proud of my voice," she'd said. *Jesus loves me, this I know.* Childlike, countrified, beautiful. Something of the music must be getting in, or the body itself is responding. I've been watching her for days for a change in expression, noting the eye-blink when Rob called and I put the phone to her ear, the one sign of response. Now I hear her machine-breathing falter, the primitive brain-breaths are softer, the lifting and filling, the falling. The body is relaxing; the music seems to be making that happen. I hit the CD player's STOP button. I want my brother Brett, who is flying in from Dallas, to get here. The phone rings and it's Joel, and they're pulling up to Village Ridge. Her breath is weakening. "Hurry," I say. "She's going."

"Mom, Mom, hold on." I'm sitting on the bed, my hand on hers. "Brett's here. Brett's coming."

Hurry–she is leaving us behind; leaving behind the butter-crank morning when she knocked out her two front teeth; leaving the four stories of the farmhouse; the root cellar's dank, where the mystery of sauerkraut happened; the crocks, the handfuls of rock salt crumbled over the shredded cabbages that would sleep for the winter in their cold brine and wake, fermented, in a different world.

It's coming, her birth into death, and this life that began in September, in another age, is ending. I hear Brett in the hall. "Hurry, Brett! Hurry!"

It is all disappearing. The honey and eggs, the windmill, the milk house, riding the black pony, the brother she adored; Luther, the best dancer, who truly loved her; the Western Dance Hall, the stars; the Depression, which taught her every lesson. *Hurry, Brett, hurry; she's taking it with her. Three cents a bushel for oats. Hurry.*

⁂

Brett runs into the room just as I hear a bubbling sound in her throat, like milk beginning to boil. The moment Brett takes her hand, the bubbling ceases. Not like the death rattle I've read of, hollow and loud, but soft, like the fizzing of milk left on the stove too long. Nights she could not sleep, she warmed milk to soothe her nerves. Brett and I look at each other. Orphans. Tears spill from his warm brown eyes, but he smiles. My brother is a man of light. When I glance over his shoulder, I see Ashley a few feet from the bed. Then Joel rushes into the room. I tell him that Mom took her last breath just as Brett walked in. "Mom took her last breath ... she waited for Brett."

Joel, who has not cried throughout this whole ordeal, begins to sob. He repeats, "Her last breath." Ashley moves closer to the bed. Let her look, I no longer care. The tears I could not stop during the last five days have dried up.

Ice Barn

We sit in the warm room, gazing at the stillness on the bed. His face swollen behind his dark glasses, Joel says, "She looked like that all week."

Our mother's mouth is open, as it has been for five days, as if drawing another breath. Stillness. Done. After all of the struggles and pleasures, all of the approximately 97,210 meals of her life; after all of the everything, we are left sitting in a silent, darkened room as though the sun has passed into the clouds. The woman who was rarely quiet while alive has been silenced. Death is, ultimately, anticlimactic. Nurse Laura walks into the room, wearing her muumuu and apron, surprisingly light on her feet for one so heavy, bending with her stethoscope over the bed. Her lank hair falls onto her face as she listens to Florence's chest.

"What are you doing there?" Joel snaps. He knows our mother disliked Laura's dictatorial bedside manner, and he tends to judge overweight people harshly. Laura more than likely weighs well over two hundred pounds. I am startled by his tone. She turns, and her intense charcoal-gray eyes focus on Joel. They have equal disdain for each other.

"I'm checking her heart in order to pronounce her dead."

I ask her if there is a heartbeat.

"No." She shakes her head and writes the date and time: 11:20 a.m., June 29, 2011. Her storm-cloud eyes are full of anger, her powerful girth ready to do battle. I step in and apologize for Joel's rudeness. She does not respond, and instead, marches out of the room.

Joel closes the door, and the three middle-aged children of the woman on the bed are alone. The three who loved her best, and yet, struggled mightily with her. Florence bequeathed her low self-esteem–the *child behind the door* syndrome–as well as her fortitude, to all her children. I envision our mother with her clip-on sunglasses anchored to the bridge of her glasses. Her blue eyes swimming over my face. All four of them, it seemed. She never wore mascara on her lashes, so her eyes missed nothing. After all the numbered lists she'd written, itemizing exactly what should be done in the event of her death, (i.e., 1. Disconnect phone; 2. Inform Social Security; 3. Find my obituary, photocopied in bottom desk drawer manila folder, etc.), I could hardly believe she wasn't watching.

Brett has already called Hospice, and Chaplain Barbara returns in her dark blue pantsuit. She reads from her prayer book. *God is faithful. He's made promises to believers.* The words do not penetrate. The window is open and the heat seeps through the screen; the drought crackles, and in Thomas Park, the dusty grapes rattle on their rusting vines. The white walls of the room look on as Brett unzips his leather pouch in which the communion wafers and grape juice have traveled from Texas. Chaplain Barbara sings "O' Precious Lord" in a rich, crystalline voice. A voice she calls God's gift. The chaplain who met my mother a month ago now speaks of the gift Florence will make of her body, and how this woman who was a teacher will give her body for study, for others to learn from. I am hearing my bargain-hunting mother say, "They cremate what's left at their expense." That *at their expense* was a selling point. "I'm at the tail end of my life." Brett has also tucked away one of her letters, which speaks of her desire for her children to be saved and to meet again in heaven. He reads aloud a tract she had cut from a *Decision* magazine.

What about the difficult times we had getting along on earth? I am thinking of my teenage self riding with Florence in the Rambler, with her staring at my halter top. Mother said, "I thought I burned that thing," and I answered with awful sarcasm, "It came back to life." She had slumped in the driver's seat. "What kind of a girl are you to talk so mouthy to your mother?" She pulled the sweater she was sitting on out from under her. "Put this on. I don't want to look at your stomach." We faced the falling sun and didn't speak. What kind of a girl was I? Then Florence let out a long breath. "There's no use talking to you. I'm going to pretend you're not here."

The more Brett reads of the Lord's promise of an afterlife, the more he repeats our mother's deepest, most desperate wish that all three of her children be saved, the more anxious I become. It's the pressure I've known since childhood. Growing up, it felt as if my brothers were given more weight. I was invisible. Joel, four years older than I, was the smartest; Brett, two years older, the kindest. We were stair steps. Brown eyes, brown hair, always holding hands, afraid to let go. Mom favored Brett, her middle child, because she had been the overlooked middle one, the shy girl who hid behind the door. Brett was the one she listened to, the one she didn't ball out. He was her *little husband.*

In a river of emotion, Brett pushes on. "You know that Mom wanted this more than anything. Her children," he says, taking off his glasses to wipe his tears. "*All her children* in heaven." His brown eyes are still those of his younger self. His voice breaks when he speaks of the Lord, and more tears pour down his face. I picture him as an 11-year-old, sitting cross-legged on the middle room floor as he carved soap men–pirates and crusaders–from the scraps of old Ivory soap stored in a Butternut coffee can. Rubbing the knees of his corduroy pants as he daydreamed. I did most of my growing up alone. Like a weed.

"It's easy to give yourself to Christ," Brett says. In our grief, Joel and I should do what would have pleased her most. What if right now I gave myself to Christ? What does it mean to give yourself away like that?

Joel excuses himself to call the funeral director. The seven hours begin now; her body needs to get to Iowa City, where they are expecting her.

Heat scorches the air, and the mucky places where mosquitoes breed have dried up as the rising temperatures break all records. Fireflies dazzle the night in numbers I've not seen since childhood. Their natural predator, the mosquito, unhatched this summer. The wild turkeys hobble between trees; the great feathered beauties, with their gobbles, grub for worms.

When Joel returns, still wearing his sunglasses, Brett passes around the thumb-sized cups of grape juices and bits of cracker. Our mother has been taken up to sing with Jesus, my brother says, and all the pain of the last seven years of her life has been washed away. She is with Grandma and Grandpa and Daddy. We sing hymns and Brett speaks of her hard life. The rock. Unbroken.

I listen to the heat in the screen window, the stillness in the room around the bed. All the dances, the proposals, the traveling. This middle child of Emily and John was admired, sought after. She knew what *it* was. She had experienced her life, unlike Johanna Pokorny, daughter of Reverend Pokorny, who had never married. I remember the reverend's quiet house in Ely, the trees hot and heavy, the thrust of leaves around the porch, the wild grape vines clinging to the rain gutters, but the house itself having a secluded air, as if pushing back the fruitfulness. Florence once complained to Johanna of being left a widow with three children, and she had responded, "At least you knew what *it* was." A man, sex, childbirth, motherhood. *It.* What could be worse than never knowing? Johanna, once called the prettiest girl in Linn County, had died a virgin.

Stillness.

⁂

I walk to the bed. She is still warm, and I kiss her forehead and smell the Moonlight Mile body lotion. My eyes keep returning to her shoes, with her footies resting in them where she last took them off, still holding the shape of her foot. Her glasses folded on the desk. The things almost cry out in their loneliness and loss. The dentures in their soaking solution. The worn underwear. Not the good clothing hanging in her closet, but the intimate things that will not be passed on to Goodwill or the Salvation Army. The blue dress she had worn to her granddaughter's wedding.

These are the first minutes of my new life, without a mother. She'd hung on to watch over us in her way, as if she knew her life shielded our lives, and now, we are next. I'm picturing the shortcut on Red Ball Road, the ice barn built into the hillside, the ice sawed from the river and pulled up the hill by the long-tongued wagon and workhorses. I never saw the gentle giants. Or the men covered in sawdust who carved the ice and salted it with rock salt. Into the huge dark barn they went and, in summer, the mammoth ice blocks would be chipped, and they would hiss and hum. That has slipped from living memory into history.

The funeral director arrives. He's a slender, thirtyish man named Adam, in dark slacks and a short-sleeved white shirt threaded with gold lines. My brothers help Adam transfer my mother from the bed onto the gurney. Then he unfolds the body bag, thick and rubbery like a scuba diver's deep-sea diving suit. He is zipping her into it, and leaves her head still showing. My brothers and I lean over to kiss her, to take a last look at our mother, the woman we thought would never die.

I keep hearing some of Florence's phrases: "Brett wants to come next summer and bring his whole gang" (wife, children). "I'm just going to sit here and keep still." "Don't just sit there like a bump on a log." "Look who's calling the kettle black." "I'm so glad my brother liked me. I'm sure he was my mother's favorite. He helped her in the garden." I will never again see the mouth that had formed those sentences. Nothing has ever felt like this, and yet, I feel nothing. "Come and I'll take care of you," she had said to me in her 88th year, after my mammogram, which had required a biopsy.

Without saying a word, we each touch a part of the gurney that carries our mother and follow Adam through the halls, passing nurses and residents who stop to watch the procession. Death and birth. Unrepeatable. We exit out a side door, into the 105 degrees. The weather we are witnessing has not been seen on this earth in millions of years. Tonight the moon will rise like clotted butter that tomorrow's terrible sun will melt. My brothers and I, the three of us, *well into Sunday,* as Joel has said, have lived long enough to witness the new age of dying cornfields, earthworms crinkling in the parched soil. I glance up the hill to Village Ridge, the chaise lounges under a canopy where the staff takes its breaks, where my mother's aide and nurse, Ashley and Squirrel, are puffing on cigarettes. The waiting hearse looks more like an eggshell-white SUV, and when the back doors open, Adam rolls the gurney in. This is the vehicle that will transport Florence to the School of Anatomy in Iowa City. We shake Adam's hand, and then he gets behind the wheel and pulls out of the parking lot. We watch the SUV cross First Avenue and then turn, disappearing in Cedar Rapids traffic over the next rise. Later, I will read the cadaver rules from the University of Iowa: how Florence will be kept moist at all times; how she'll be embalmed with a light mist of glycerin and ethyl alcohol; how, to touch her, you will have to wear disposable gloves; and, after working on her, you will mist her again from the spray pump filled with glycerin.

Joel says, "That's it. End of story."

This flat asphalt parking lot is the final stop of Florence's journey.

I look up at the window of what had been my mother's breezeless room. The breath of life is everything.

⁂

The Deeded Body Program speaks of the study of human anatomy as "indispensable to medical education" and there being "a continual need for these gifts." Medical colleges can't purchase corpses for study and, in the past, gravediggers would sell their night labors in the cemetery to doctors and scientists. I think of stories I've heard of medical students naming their cadavers *Zsa Zsa* and *Deep Throat,* and making jokes about them. Surely my mother had heard those stories as well. Her belief that nothing should be wasted was ingrained, and it hurt her to see the new disposable world of junk. Even her husk would not go to waste. She'd already signed the Deed of Disposition with the Department of Anatomy and Cell Biology. "At the time of death, the person in charge of the donor's affairs should select and notify a funeral director and make arrangements to transport the body to Iowa City." The family won't be told of the gift's use; neither will they be told if the body has cancer or any other pathology. A body is unacceptable only if an autopsy has been performed, or if there's been terrible trauma, such as a car accident, a contagious disease, or weight issue, whether overweight or underweight. Yes, they still wanted her at 98, three months shy of 99.

⁂

We sit in chairs assembled for the bedside vigil, staring into space in Florence's old room. Joel, who has always been the toughest of us, wipes away tears. The tears stop and start again. So this is the day it happened. I try to see the day our mother was born. A world without antibiotics, without electricity, a world of outhouses and ice barns, of long winters and shivering, of kerosene wicks to trim and cobs to carry from the corncrib to the woodbox.

Brett offers the first words to break the spell. "Should we go get something to eat? Maybe the Maid-Rite Café?" He's been traveling since 4 a.m.

"You don't want to sit in a restaurant and waste this perfectly beautiful day," Joel says, already on his feet. The eldest. In charge. "Mom would want us to go on a picnic."

It's true. The tradition in our family is to go on picnics in the summer. To enjoy the Iowa countryside parks, to relax and eat together from Florence's brown and white tin picnic box. On the second to last picnic of her life, my brothers had driven her to a breathtaking lake in Palo, five miles from the nuclear plant. Returning, the skies turned greenish-black, the air looked as if it were on fire, and the tails of the black clouds followed them, about to touch down. My brothers in the front seat, Joel driving, and Florence sitting in back. Tornado weather, the mix of black and green in the sky. The dementia mother screamed and then she cried. "Like a child," Joel said. "Just like a frightened child."

Hy-Vee

Hy-Vee is the premier supermarket chain in Iowa and that's where we've driven, as Florence makes her last car trip. At the meat counter, Joel is quizzing the counter help about whether the shrimp comes from the Gulf of Mexico or a fish farm, and the beef, whether or not it's Iowa raised and Iowa corn-fed. Joel orders a half pound of the jumbo and a half pound of the popcorn shrimp. "The sirloin. Which cut do you recommend for grilling?" my brother asks. "I've traveled from California for a cut of Iowa beef." The white-aproned counterman with sandy hair and glasses, who reminds me of the funeral director, seems pleased to be asked to bring his expertise to bear. He recommends the flank steak for the grill or the rib eye. "Is that cut from the eye of your best prime rib roast?" Joel asks. "You bet" is the answer. Brett is after the kielbasa sausages. He, too, strikes up a conversation with the counter help. The rings of sausage glint pinkly, coiled into their pyramids. The air conditioning must be turned up to frigid–the whole store is the temperature of a meat locker. I wander through the salad bar, picking out the olives and sun-dried tomatoes. I have no questions regarding the origins of the pickled beets. At least they have not suffered the slaughterhouse, going from sentient being to veal. Yet I admire how my brothers pepper the air with inquiries. Wherever they go, they're prone to striking up friendly conversations. They are now in Produce, selecting tomatoes and sweet corn.

⁂

Palisades State Park is where my brothers have decided we'll go for our picnic. We're twelve miles north of Cedar Rapids and five miles from the farm where we grew up when Joel exits off the interstate. He turns onto the blacktop that takes us into the park. The road curves past jack oak and hickory, the leaves grayed with platters of dust. There's no one else at this picnic site near the Cedar River on a weekday afternoon. Two years ago, the river crested, a one-hundred-year flood, and now the stagnant current hardly moves the silty, muddy water along. The mucky shallows, a place for cranes to hunt with their dagger-like bills.

I set the picnic table while Brett builds the charcoal briquettes into a pyramid and douses it with lighter fluid. Joel walks to his car trunk for his mango tea jar. There is no breeze from the trees and it is hot. He sips from his jar as he strolls back to the picnic table. He's donned a sun visor hat. Once, Joel bought Mom a box of chocolates and gave them to her with the receipt still in the bag. She scoured the receipt and saw that Joel had purchased the chocolates in a liquor store. "Whiskey!" she said, as if whiskey were the filthy bathwater of Lucifer, funneled into an expensive bottle. And they were lovely chocolates from the master chocolatiers. Caramel éclairs, crème brûlée.

Joel was sure she would make it to 100; we all thought she would. For him, this is our mother's sudden death.

⁂

In the afternoon light, I see the wear on my brothers' faces and feel it on my own. Brett mans the grill, turning the sausages and rib eyes. First, Joel spears tomatoes and shrimp onto a skewer, followed by onions and peppers. I already smell the corn on the cob, wrapped in tin foil and laid on the smoking coals. It has been a lifetime since all three of us were here together. The trees and leaves still smell like spit, like they did when I was 9. I remember how my brothers hiked up the rocks, faster and farther up and up, tugging on roots that made loops between stones. Feverish, all I wanted was to lie down. Still, my brothers climbed, and my mother, behind me, urged me to keep going.

"Do you think I could motivate Rob?" Joel asks. Now he's cutting a ripe Iowa tomato, salting it with a Hy-Vee individual salt-and-pepper packet. He has hundreds of these stowed in a plastic bucket that travels in the car with him. Brett slides in next to Joel on the male side of the table.

"What do you mean by *motivate*?" I ask. "He's extraordinarily productive. He writes every day ..."

Joel slides off his sunglasses, letting them hang from a long string guard around his neck. "So, you estimate Rob spends how many hours a day writing poetry?" He rubs at the corners of his eyes.

"I'd say four hours, and then he edits our literary journal."

"What, maybe two hours more a day? That's six hours, and what does he do with the rest of his time?"

"He has to read submissions and he goes to the gym. He's very disciplined."

Joel's reddened eyes appear amber; they've faded from the dark brown of childhood. Like my own have. "I can see he's strong. Would he be willing to do construction work? It pays the bills."

I notice pink suns jittering on the edges of the leaves. "But he's clumsy. His father is too. He's done some freelance editing," I offer.

"Freelance editing? How much does he charge an hour?"

"You charge by the manuscript, and most writers are poor." I'm watching the cranes fly to a sandbar in the middle of the river.

"If he did this editing for hire each day like his poetry, he might contribute. Explain what would prevent him from that," Joel continues. Brett says nothing, letting Joel ask the questions, but he's listening intently. He stands up so that he can cut a piece of smoldering sausage, and tastes it. "That's good," he says, smacking his lips.

I don't answer. A red heat flushes my forehead and cheeks. Our mother has just died.

"It looks as though he eats a lot," Joel comments, as he cuts two tomatoes with a plastic fork, fifty extras in his car in his Hy-Vee bucket, and transfers them to his mouth. "Who pays for food?"

"His parents give him some money." Flies walk delicately around a tomato slice, gleaming and freshly cut, on a paper plate. Like a moist kiss.

"Is that right? How much?"

"Four hundred a month."

"So, does he eat more than four hundred a month? Mom mentioned that she never saw anyone eat like him. Now, who pays for shampoo and toothpaste?"

"I do, but he does all the cooking. He does the grocery shopping and the laundry. He mops the floor before I get home."

"So he does some household chores. Give me kind of a capsule view of what his day looks like from the time he gets up."

"Joel, please, I feel like I'm on trial." I take a drink of water and eat three olives, and look to Brett, my kindly middle brother, for support. He tugs thoughtfully on his beard and then cups his chin in his hand, staring out at the brown, poisoned river. The chocolate sludge dragging the current.

"I'm just asking a simple question. About what time does he get up?"

"I go to work at 10:00, and he gets up after I leave."

Joel drinks from his mango tea jar, a smile crossing his lips. "Not an early riser."

They are ganging up on me. Like the nightmare day of the rock climb, the car barely stopping before my brothers burst out of the Rambler and scrambled up the trails of beaten dirt, their feet raining rocks down. Joel and Brett were burr-headed, their scalps nicked from fresh haircuts, Mother barbering each on the step ladder in the farmhouse kitchen. The sun hurt my eyes, a headache began blistering my forehead, and still my brothers yelped and climbed higher. From behind, Florence kept prodding me to hurry. "I don't feel well," I told her, but she sighed in exasperation. "Don't spoil your brothers' time."

They were explorers. Balboa and Magellan. Shivering in the 90 degrees of July, the heat coming from every direction. My head hard to hold up. Keep going. The dirt trail dragged me along. Rocks oozed heat. Then we were going down, and in a burst I ran until, panting, I came to the locked Rambler and threw myself down in the dirt beside the back tire. Ants crawled on me. They climbed up my back. I heard their ant voices, but their voices, like my brothers', sounded muffled, a long way off. No one would believe that I was burning up. I had scarlatina. I wanted water–not river mud.

I drift as Joel quizzes me. My mind wanders. I can't focus on Rob's employment prospects; that would be like trying to motivate a refrigerator.

The old farmers fished here for carp and blue gills. My grandfather brought me here when I was 4, and we drove in his Hudson on Red Ball Road and entered Palisades Park on a secret path remembered only in dead men's dreams. Happy to be with my grandfather, I wanted to go everywhere with him.

My oldest brother is still questioning me. "Mom scrimped and saved, didn't even buy herself new underwear. She worried about Rob not working and wondered if there was anything he could do. I still think construction."

"All of the construction in Manhattan is tied up in unions," I say, trying to bat the questions away. The buzzing of horseflies.

"I don't think so. There's always room for an independent contractor. What about house painting?"

I think of the Albanian immigrant who painted my East Village apartment; he was fast, professional, and took cash only. I can't conceive of Rob in the business of gathering ladders and drop cloths, buckets, and paints, and primers.

"Well, what about gym work? Personal trainer?"

The sweet corn is ready. Out come the Hy-Vee butter pads. Joel gnaws on his corn on the cob; Brett chews his grilled kielbasa sausage. I'm eating the sweet corn and shrimp, happy that the subject of Rob seems to have been exhausted. I think of Florence's look-who's-calling-the-kettle-black expression. What about Joel's ex-wife, Daisy? When Joel married Daisy in the Philippines, there were ten bridesmaids and ten groomsmen, and the petite bride wore her glossy black hair swept up and woven with flowers as though a towering Marie Antoinette wig, and a gown of bows and taffeta and lace scallops, and a train so long it took four nephews to hold it above the red runner of carpet. Joel, the bridegroom, and the only Westerner in the wedding party, wore the traditional white Nehru jacket and slacks. Joel mailed our mother the marriage announcement that had appeared in the local paper, which listed the ten bridesmaids and ten groomsmen, their formal names in the Spanish tradition, two first names and two last names; and a description of the finery worn by everyone, including the three flower girls and three ring bearers. "Honestly," our mother had said afterwards, "you would think a king and queen were getting married. Ten bridesmaids! Like royalty. And Joel had to buy her father a pair of shoes."

Always the farm-girl flourish.

Florence. I hear her: "I didn't go to church this morning because my car didn't start. When I go to church on Sunday, the month is divided into weeks. If I don't go to church, the month is just a blob."

I think of our mother's 1957 diary. What would the Florence of 1957 think if she had been given a vision of her adult children?

Feb 11, 1957

> *Joel is to be a lollipop in a school program. I'm to sew pajamas for him–first I must color red stripes on material, iron, and then sew.*

Blame It on the Hour

The first leg of the flight out of LaGuardia starts late, the American Airlines plane grounded because of mechanical failure–the flight canceled. There's a mad rush to another gate and hours pass. It is July and my mother has been dead a year. Again, I am flying to Iowa. After waiting and waiting, I am rerouted to Kansas City, Missouri. Finally we board, and the plane lifts through a haze thick as beer malt. Soon, New York is so small I could step on it. The ground below recedes. White silos of chemicals and swimming pools of sewage. The jittering interstates. The crowded, sour East an anthill I could kick at–stone, lathe, and plaster; glass and steel in granules.

My brothers are already in Cedar Rapids with the urn that contains my mother's ashes, her grit and bone fragments returned to us by the School of Anatomy. The day after tomorrow we'll bury what's left of her next to Philip, our father, whose bones have moldered a half a century in Rogers' Grove, awaiting his wife. We've invited the remnants of the Telecky and Buresh clan, the older generation. We'll never know where Florence went in the past twelve months, or how she was used; the mother whose body had fed us was perhaps a cadaver for a medical student or a classroom dissection; perhaps her bones were ground and sold to dental practices, her marrow packed into patients' jaws. I think of her limbs sawed off and my mother calling out to them. I wonder what the cold sleep in the morgue felt like for the girl who liked summer best; for the woman who, in winter, wore two scarves, one tied under her chin and the other wrapped like a bandanna, Apache-style, around her forehead.

In my lap there's a stack of Florence's letters; they are tinder, flammable, and I'm afraid to read them. Afraid of the loneliness, of her almost-beautiful handwriting, still strong and legible in her 90s. I open 1998. Oct. 8. "Outside of my children–I have never given or exchanged gifts with 'mere' friends. If I had, they certainly wouldn't have been lavish ones. I have kept my friends through letters, Christmas cards, and phone calls (if in vicinity). PS: I wish you'd take that black stuff out of your eyes. You're not a girl anymore. I know I might as well be talking to the wind."

I recognize her language and her love of dashes and quotes to indicate emphasis. There is a clipping taped to the sheet: "Too frequent hair washing and blow-drying leads to hair loss."

I listen to the safety instructions–a piped-in woman's voice that the male flight attendant pantomimes to. Exits and flotation devices. I wonder what it feels like when something does happen, when the skin of the plane breaks open in midair and there is only a sea of green corn under you; what it's like going down with the rest of the coach passengers; strangers, although your legs rub as if you were lovers. Communal death seems not your own, yet better than a natural death, the most horrific of all. Like Florence's.

March 8, 2011. Florence wakes at 10:00 p.m. on a Thursday evening and is thinking of writing to me. Most likely she had tucked herself in at 9:00. I am several states away when I should be close at hand. Always broke, endlessly throwing my money away. "I haven't seen any promises with your present 'checkers.' Maybe they just <u>keep</u>

your ideas and use some of them for themselves. Don't always accept any of these 'downbeats.' I would never have written a story that would 'die' after the event. I had to go to college piecemeal! As I have said over & over, nobody reads books–not here either! Except exotic ones."

"I have always enjoyed the 'work' I was doing through those years! Now it is 'dead' for me. Now that I've reread what I wrote, I wonder if I should send it?? Tear it up after you read it!!"

"Blame it on the Hour!"

"I'll try the bed now!"

"Take care of your life–when will it be healed??"

⁕ ⁕

The beverage cart jiggles down the aisle, as do the air waitresses, whose smiles look as if asteroids have gone down in their mouths. "Ma'am, what may I get you?" I'm well into the age of *ma'am*, of *hag* and *crone*, and I hate it. *Ma'am,* the thrower often my age or older. I've never called anyone *ma'am* in my life, unless provoked first. I have a name; call me *nothing*. Below the silver belly of the plane, I see the Midwest, the flatlands, the prairie scraped of its seven-foot grasses and furrowed into fields of corn and soybeans. The drought this year is even worse than last, and instead of the lush green of crops and trees, the earth is parched. Florence lived three more months. Her thinking continued to fray, the written word that had always tumbled easily from her pen became a jungle of unrecognizable vines and creepers, but she hung on to the exclamation point like a staff in shifting canopy, a solidity. "I appreciate you and Rob taking me out to dinner Sunday–even more than the bracelet (which is beautiful)–but the dinner was from 'yourselves,' not from a store. Someday you'll understand." It is the phrase "someday you'll understand" that haunts me.

In the last months of her life, she had eaten in the dining room at Village Ridge. Assigned to a table shared with three others, the meals that should have nourished my mother had tormented her. Apparently, peer pressure ends only when you do. Florence, the teacher, the director of plays, the Red Cross worker who coordinated entertainment, could think of nothing to say. In her room she hit her head, palm against her forehead, calling it a "dumb head," but still the thoughts did not flow freely. In her last notes, her handwriting had not yet faltered, but there were blanks, underlines where words were missing. She was sure one of the women at her dining room table asked to be moved because Florence had forgotten words with which to make conversation.

1. Move me out of table where I sit.
2. I tried to be____can't hear. (tonite she didn't
    want that folded paper
Names and places of places out east and south
I've asked for those. Not fancy stuff.
3. I worked with hundreds of people.
Embarrased??

I can hardly bear to read this, how she struggled in her loneliness for her mind. I unfold a photo that my brother has scanned into his computer and e-mailed. I've printed it out on 8 ½ by 11" paper, and from the tiny snapshot taken decades ago under a distant sun, I've enlarged the moment. I search for hidden details. It is of my tall, handsome uncle Fred, a cousin, my mother, and Luther. The four of them are posing on the farmhouse lawn. It must be the season of white shoes, as they are all wearing them. My mother's dress is shorter than that of her cousin, who is a plain, bespectacled girl. Luther is taller by half a head than my mother. I can see them dancing together easily, eyes looking into eyes. Luther wears a printed tie, which the breeze ruffles onto its side. Florence is standing almost hip to hip with him, her body turned. He keeps his hands in his pockets; her left hand is resting on his shoulder, a gesture that seems familiar and intimate. It's a Sunday afternoon, and summer. An orchard tree drops its branches across the fence like hair. Aroma of ripening apples. Daddy-longlegs climbing between leaves. I think of the hundreds I used to see when I cut through the cornfields–amber bodies, an eye attached to elegant, wiry limbs. I loved them. Abide with me, daddy-longlegs, and ants, shiny and plump.

The hardest year of her life. "Stephanie understands."

Kansas City, another delay, and I am told there are no flights to Cedar Rapids. I'm rerouted to Des Moines, and from there I will make my connection. American Airlines planes are overworked, all on the verge of collapse. More mechanical difficulties; our plane does not pass inspection, but another plane is being found and brought 'round. I flip through the notebook, so old its spirals are rusted.

February 18

Phil was to give a talk at a school at Arlington Heights so he left this afternoon. He and I were to give devotions for Mariners–so I had to give it alone.

February 22

Phil didn't come home for supper Wed nite nor tonite.

February 27

Phil drove to Chicago to see his folks again. He stayed there overnight last nite– and all day today. I expected him for supper but he called around 7:00 from his folks that he was bringing Uncle Morris. They arrived around 11:00.

April 8, 1956

Brett still couldn't go to Sunday school today–he still has a little cough. Poor darling sees the other children playing outdoors and he doesn't fuss that he can't go.

There are lists of chores: clean house, wash dishes, bake and frost birthday cake, make supper, wash supper dishes, bake rolls and kolaches, while Phil goes to Joliet to plant trees.

My father. In the memories (two) I have of him, he's already receded into the distance. My father was taking my brothers to check deer-feeding stations; the three of them had already gotten into the black pickup that belonged to the State of Illinois Department of Conservation. I wanted to go too. I pressed my face to the window, watching the black truck back out of the driveway. I cried inconsolably.

Another fragment. My brothers and I standing on a grassy knoll next to a tall building. Maybe it was only a building of six stories, but to a 3-year-old it may as well have been a skyscraper. Our mother leaning out the open second-story window, encouraging us to say hello to Daddy. *We miss you, Daddy. Get well soon.* Children were not allowed inside. Like a dream in green and white, it's so far off. I know it's a hospital and my father is lying inside on a bed in the room where my mother is. The general practice doctors told my mother that Phil could live for years with his heart condition, if he were careful. The heart specialist, Dr. Nelson, said later that he didn't expect my father to grow old. The hole in his heart was shrinking and he had to keep breathing deeper to feed his body with oxygen.

October 27th

Phil gone every evening this week.

October 29th

Phil left for duck area again tonite. He is to return around Dec. 1st. There are 10-degrees-below-zero days.

In my mother's diary of 1956, the last full year of my father's life, we see him coming and going, giving speeches, working for the Wildlife Bureau as a conservation biologist, leaving for deer hunts and pheasant feedings, missing suppers, missing church. It is my mother there with the endless runny noses of three children. The terrible coughs, the fevers of 102 degrees. *Phil left for Lansing, Michigan, this morning.* Another day to take the children to church alone. *Phil gone for a dove count.* We see her at church and baby showers. A Who's New Luncheon, the quaint trappings of the post-war era, the making of the baby boom generation. We see the word *alone.*

> *March 4th*
>
> *Friday nite I went to the doctor. I've been having nausea a lot–had pains where my operation is–have been having headaches. He said that it was probably from my nerves & gave me some nerve pills.*

She is referring to her Caesarean scar; the vertical cut was made three times, from her navel to her pubic mound. My mother had suffered post-partum depression, what she called her nervous breakdown, following Joel's birth. Her scar-gutted stomach that split her down the middle horrified me.

* *

The plane to Des Moines is ready for boarding. I slide the envelopes back in the pouch that holds more envelopes. I close the year 1956 back into the notebook with the rusted spirals. Light from that year is traveling through space; life is still going on there but unreachable from here. There, Joel comes down with a fever, breaking out with measles, his face and shoulders spotted by a dark red rash; hot days with only fans, sweating days, damp days, clothes not drying on the line. *Teppy* standing up by herself in the tub, good and lovable as always. I am *Steff, Teppy, Stephy,* and *Tep.* Florence is canning nine quarts of applesauce. Phil is tightening jars. *Steff to doctor. She has impetigo on buttocks. I have some on my arms and fingers.*

At last we are boarding the flight to Des Moines, the penultimate leg of the endless journey. Impatient to find our seats, each of us clutches our boarding passes. Soon we'll land in drought country. The creeks that etch their way through the ash-colored earth are only a dribble now, as if fire had burned through their beds.

In Des Moines I connect to a puddle-jumper and am about to board, when the flight attendant tells me the boarding pass I was given in Kansas City is no good. That flight has been canceled. My heart sinks. I tell her that every one of my connections since LaGuardia has been canceled; I tell her I am burying my mother and need to get on that plane. A six-hour trip has now taken fifteen hours. Finally, a seat is found for me.

It is almost midnight when the lights of Cedar Rapids lift themselves from the prairie dark. The ground that the plane will land on was purchased from my Buresh relatives. I know this countryside; this is my hallowed ground. We fly over the farmhouse, the oaks and hickories; my 7- and 10- and 12-year-old selves are down there climbing the slats of the corncrib, standing in the farm wind, poking the wasp's nest with a stick. There's the garden, with its silty stalks of sweet corn and white squash blossoms haunting the green vines; Jack, the donkey, breaking out of his pasture, romping and hee-hawing at 5 a.m. Where does he think he's running to? Freedom? From the smell of the saddle, the wound of confinement. I understand now, after all the water has flowed under the bridge, how precious our beginnings are.

This is the first time I've flown in to Iowa that my mother is not alive. I can almost hear the rustling of cornstalks and baked weeds. The fried Queen Anne's lace. Florence no longer knows Moscow, Idaho, or how she hated rattlesnakes, the trillions of galaxies, the Red Cross.

She has entered the mysterious black hole of life after death; she's been dissected like a warty frog. Those dances with Luther under the thick Iowa stars have vanished.

⁂

My best friend, Cynthia, stands up in the waiting area and opens her arms to hug me; her white teeth blaze in a smile that lights up her lovely face. She wears her fine brown hair almost to her waist and parted in the middle, like a whole generation of girls once did. We laugh and chatter into a wave of dry heat. She is a brilliant woman, a pioneer in the field of in vitro fertilization.

We discuss the man whom Cynthia is seeing. "At this age," she laughs, "I'm being used for sex."

I laugh too. "Take it as a compliment." And it is a compliment.

We drive the River-to-River Highway to Iowa City. Three years ago, the 100-year flood ripped willows from the Iowa River's banks; fawns, separated from their mothers, swam for their lives, water cresting over the highway. We pass through towns still soiled from river murk, the dirty yellow x's for houses to be demolished. Still no street lamps. A gray zone, as if the old farms had walked into town–the weathered, the parched, and the rusted.

"It seems you get your chance when you're young. I go into any diner on a Sunday morning and see tables of women our age–long-haired, good-looking women–never a man or wedding ring in sight," Cynthia says.

Tonight I'll sleep in Iowa City and tomorrow my friend will drive me to Marion/Cedar Rapids to meet my brothers, who are staying at the Super 80. I'll dream I'm still flying, I'll dream of a summer ice harvest above the dam, a picnic of wild plums and wild grapes, heat breathing from the trees. I'll be holding a pewter jelly spoon, the one with the pattern of milkweed.

••

I meet my brothers in Marion at the Hy-Vee. It must be our comfort station, as we are once again strolling the deli with forks in hand. Joel is wearing his Bermuda shorts, a red T-shirt, sunglasses, and a visor. He's deeply tanned and has just returned from Southeast Asia, where he's been for the last six months. Part of that time he spent riding a motorcycle with Somai, his new Thai girlfriend, through the mountain terrain and trails of northern Thailand and Vietnam. Somai has had little schooling, as her high school years were spent slaving 12 hours a day, 7 days a week in a factory to support her birth family, and then a husband, who deserted her and their daughter. She must appreciate the kindness and intelligence of my brother. I am happy for him.

"Okay, kiddo, get yourself a salad. Here's the plan," Joel says, filling his pockets with butter pats and salt and peppers. "We're going to be cleaning out Mom's storage this afternoon. And tonight we're going for dinner at The Lighthouse, where Mom and Luther used to dance. The same family owns it now as then, only a different generation."

Brett is looking over the watermelon slices. Unlike last summer, he appears relaxed, in his T-shirt and shorts. I heap my Styrofoam container with vegetables and fruits because in Iowa you do as the Iowans do; you load your plate. On go peppers and tomatoes and cucumbers, but no olives, no artichoke hearts, no edamame. There's more iceberg lettuce here in one salad bar than you see in an entire New York supermarket, where healthier spinach, kale, radicchio, and endive are the more popular choices. No bottles of balsamic vinegar and olive oil; instead, there are vats of blue cheese and ranch dressing with gravy ladles boating in them and spill-trails over the watermelon slices. My brothers' salads hardly fit into their containers, which bulge like overstuffed suitcases. Yet, I like being in this store, where the Iowans pass by, farmer-tanned, showing the white marks made by collars and sleeves, fleshy, friendly, and far from the trendy, edgy crowds of Manhattan. I like being with my brothers. Once again there are the three of us, who, as children, held hands tightly. Our Sunday-school teacher told Florence that we would not let go of each other's hands. I try to picture what my life would have been like had I not left Iowa, hadn't hitchhiked, hadn't been shot. If I'd become a teacher as my mother had wanted me to, married, had children, perhaps a teacher husband; if I'd had a home to offer my mother in her old age. I can't even conjure that scenario.

We drive to Marion Storage. A retired couple runs the operation out of their backyard, having turned their half-acre into storage units of varying sizes, i.e., from one-car garages to doghouses. My brothers have worked all morning separating Florence's possessions into four destinations: the donations to The Salvation Army and Goodwill; the antiques and family heirlooms to be driven to Uncle Fred's son, Fred Jr., in Dallas; the heirlooms my brothers and I each want; and the resting place of Florence's treasured junk–the dumpster.

The door to the storage unit is open, revealing box upon box. Two industrial-sized dumpsters, large as ladies-in-waiting, stand nearby. The round oak table and wooden chairs, built by our great-grandfather, sit in the middle of the asphalt lot. Brett parks the U-Haul with the bed of the truck facing the table. This is the table of our childhood, the one we ate at in the farmhouse, with Florence at the head (if round can have a head), Joel across from me, and Brett across from our mother. We each pull out a chair and take our seats under the blue sky and sun.

There's Florence rushing by, dressed in her teaching skirt and sweater, muttering *something is burning*. It's not the midday sun, the sizzling 100 degrees, but maybe Malt-O-Meal or Cream of Wheat or oatmeal. Or is she frying slabs of cornmeal mush until it's crisp and delicious? *Pass the Karo syrup. Don't forget to take your vitamin pill.*

My brothers and I are having our last meal at the oak table. I watch the bread-loaf clouds drifting by. The table will be departing Iowa, where it once lived as a tree, leaving us forever and going to Texas, as are the wooden chairs, the antique velvet rocker, and loveseats, all of which Florence refinished herself. Scrolled walnut arms and legs, cushions covered in plush maroon velvet–the jewels of our living room. *You people will throw away everything.* (I can hear Florence's words.)

In this humble storage with the cheapest available rates, our mother's antiques and household possessions have been stored for the last year. After we finish eating, Brett lowers the gate and opens the back end of the U-Haul that he'll be driving to Dallas. His first stop will be at Fred Jr.'s. As a boy, we called him *Fritzie,* and bowed to his preternatural brilliance. He was allergic to pollen of every kind–milkweed, sumac, wild onion, lamb's ear–and was forever blowing his nose. Given the old antique party-line phone of our grandparents, he wired it into a shock box to use on my brothers. The phone bell rang when it shocked you. Fritzie had so many degrees that Florence called him a professional student. The last degree made him a lawyer, and then, as they used to say, he *buckled down* and became vice president of Texas Instruments. Like my uncle and aunt, Fred Jr.'s love of antiques was legendary.

Brett climbs into the bed of the U-Haul. Behind him are the velvet loveseats facing each other, the solid wood buffet, the heirloom embossed with the Lord's Prayer in Czech. Joel and I continue to sit at the table while Brett picks from the cardboard boxes. This will be the fourth and final culling of Florence's possessions. *Her life,* as she often put it. Already gone are the plastic tub containers, the 40 bags of them; already gone, the plastic forks and knives, the Dairy Queen's red, long-handled ice cream spoons, the rags. Mother, who saved everything, including ice cream, put aside for a special occasion until it had turned gummy, the vanilla yellowing, our root beer floats often made with freezer-burnt ice cream.

"Okay, Joel and Stephanie," Brett says. "I'm going to hold things up. You decide whether it goes or stays or if you'd like to keep it."

In his hands there's the wooden bowl that held desert rocks. First it belonged to Grandmother, who kept it on a shelf in the front room. In the hot sunlight, I still feel the mysteries of the bowl, with its woven wood, speaking to me of faraway places.

"That was Grandma's," I say. "I have always loved it, but I have no room for it."

"Joel? The dumpster then?"

He nods.

Brett holds up the country-school English primer, with a medieval knight on its cover, the one with pages spilling out and a rubber band around it. Inside are Rip Van Winkle and Pandora's Box, the Seven Thieves, the shrewish tongue of Dame Van Winkle, and Pandora, looking at the flower faces in the carved box, admiring her own apple-blossom cheeks. Inside, she's sure, exists a world where you can eat your fill from trees–fig and olive, peach and apple; a world where everyone stays young and spring water tumbles out of rocks. The primer I pored over endlessly during farm summers, marooned, with no books to be had from the school library; summers I spent scouring the bookshelves.

"I want to keep that," I say.

Since Joel has no home, and I live in a five-story walk-up tenement, what the two of us want to keep will be consigned to a tiny $10-a-month unit, the cheapest he happened upon, in nearby Palo, by the nuclear plant. We are downsizing storage units.

One by one, the objects I considered beautiful as a child are being held up in Brett's hand. The hand-painted vase that stood half my height, the plumes of pampas grass; those too are heading south, along with the crescent moon knick-knack with wooden stairway and a wooden star.

The painting of the three horses hung on the front room wall. The room was closed for the winter to save on fuel, and I would stare through the glass doors, into the cold, at the painting in its round walnut frame. I would gaze at the horses' manes, their nostrils flaring; one terrified eye each, black as well water. I could hear them whinnying–three horses struggling head to head as if bridled or drowning, and behind them, the sky on fire. I wanted to save them from the smoke of whatever barn or woods were burning. I willed them to escape; I wished to hear them softly neigh as they galloped free. I wanted the impossible to happen, but it never did. And now the three horses, painted in the 19th Century, will travel to the Sun Belt's 21st Century. *Goodbye, horses. I once believed you more human than any human.*

Now comes my mother's costume jewelry; pounds of bright cheap beads in all colors. Chocolate boxes overflowing with pearls. I think back to all the visits in which she'd begged me to take some of the beads home with me. *Honestly, all my beautiful beads. Beads dress up any outfit.* I took the seed pearl necklace that Luther had given her, the Black Hills gold necklace, the gold compact with FT (Florence Telecky) engraved on the back, with a powder puff and the remnants of 75-year-old rouge inside.

The cedar chest with Florence's wedding dress will go into the Palo storage, as well as the never-used sterling silver set, a wedding gift from our grandparents to our parents. I tell Brett that my niece Amanda should have the sterling silver, but he shakes his head, as she already has a set from her other grandmother.

Joel carries the boxes of our mother's purses to the dumpster. Her voice echoes. *While you're here, don't you want some of my purses? What will people think of you carrying such a big bag all stuffed?*

Here is the geisha girl in burgundy kimono waving a fan and the souvenir salt-and-pepper shakers, most of them having lost their mates.

The gravy pitcher.

The mirror from over the buffet, and the buffet whose legs I had wiped with a vinegar rag, the buffet I had sat on, talking to myself in the mirror. The mirror, no one wants; too cumbersome, no room.

⁂

The sun is pitched dizzily overhead as we get to the final box of Florence's possessions. Brett, still in the back of the U-Haul, holds up a white platter trimmed in gold. Joel and I sit at the oak table, now surrounded by three distinct piles of boxes, readied for their separate fates, the largest grouping bound for the Marion Storage dumpster.

"That's from Grandma's best china set," I say. "Remember how she kept them in the corner cupboard by the sink?"

"And she brought them out only for Thanksgiving," Joel adds. "I'd like to keep those."

I picture the corner cupboard by the sink, where the sunset shone in the kitchen window; I see Grandma perched on her step ladder, reaching up to the second shelf and handing me down the precious plates to set on the table. Platters and gravy boats stamped with a gold rosebud, coffee cups and saucers to match. How vulnerable the dishes seem, exposed to the sun like unearthed bones. If one of them should fall, the asphalt would smash it.

"Two more items," Brett says, wiping his forehead. "Then we're finished." He reaches into the last cardboard box, and I wonder what piece of our childhood will emerge. It's a painting in an ornate lime-green frame. I take a deep breath, immediately recognizing it.

The painting was stored in Grandma's attic against the stacked bed-boards. Summers, I was charged with spring-cleaning the attic windows, ridding the sills of flies, those pocketfuls of pests that had wintered between two panes of glass. I would slide the storm window up and in came the sultry farm air, and the pile of flies would begin to stir, waking from their long naps. I would hear them buzz and watch them stumble drunkenly on their feelers before testing their wings and flying off. The attic air always stuffy with the packed and closeted; what great-grandparents and aunts and uncles had left behind–Boy Scout uniforms, old mattresses, patchwork quilts, and feather pillows. Here were the ancient flat irons and tuneless piano; the song of the forgotten vibrated in the dead air, under the bare rafters that flypaper and dried onions dangled from. I would wipe the painting's frame and then the glass with a vinegar rag. Full of romance that hinted at immodesty–no wonder it did not find a place on the downstairs walls. A girl in a gauzy green dress, seated at a piano, holding a long-stemmed rose. She isn't playing anymore, although you can hear the tinkling keys. All she can do is stare sleepily at the rose. The flower will fall from her hand when the next moment happens. The piano teacher, the giver of the rose, whose back is turned, stands in the doorway in his apricot-colored pants. I used to dream up the two of them walking free of the frame; he, taking her hand and leading her out of the farmhouse, past the chicken coop and milk house, past the long-tongued wagon and windmill. The two hiding in the shagbark pines, the hairy trunks and rusty needles befriending them. And now, a half-century later, the two of them are unchanged.

"This is an antique and should go to Fred Jr.," Brett says, carrying the green frame deeper into the U-Haul.

Wait, I almost say, but realize the lovers will have a better home with my cousin than at the Palo storage shed.

As I watch the painting vanish into the U-Haul, I see the last of the farmhouse going with it: the high ceilings and fields, the grape arbor, the soybean bin, the root cellar, the banister, the summer kitchen, the furrows so deep and soft, my grandmother's lace tablecloths.

Then Brett sets my mother's last possession on the table–the brown and white tin picnic basket with wood handles. A half-century of picnics hides inside that rusted tin. Our father must have eaten liverwurst sandwiches wrapped in wax paper from that basket. Ellis Park, Stone City, Dixon, Chicago, Riverview Park, Pinicon Ridge, Lake Macbride. Forests of green, park after park. Even battered and rusted, the basket had gone on picnics in Florence's 98th year.

Joel speaks up. "I don't have the heart to throw that away. Let's take it to Palo."

Surely the picnic box should be buried with Florence's urn.

THE LIGHTHOUSE

Tonight my brothers are treating me to dinner at The Lighthouse, a supper club where Luther had often taken Florence. We park the U-Haul and stroll through the courtyard toward the restaurant. Crickets are rubbing their wings in full throb tonight. As we walk through the forest of *chirring*, the hairs on my body rise. Like the summer nights on the farm, dew wetting the grass and the stars shivering, everything yet to be.

Next to the entrance, a blue and white lighthouse stands like a piece of oversized lawn furniture. All the times we heard Florence say *Luther and I ate and danced here; he was the best dancer, musical like his whole family,* and yet none of us have ever eaten here until now. Florence, the working single mother of three, would not have thrown away money for a luxury meal. Iowa is not a state known for its fine dining, although the Czechs of my grandmother's and great-aunt's generations were food magicians. They knew how to breathe life into flour and yeast and almond paste, into apricots and baking powder and eggs. Their nicked fingers brought forth perfect strudel and rye bread and dumplings and crepes and kolaches and marzipan cookies. My mother's generation learned Jiffy Mix and canned tamales, while my generation cooks and eats from the microwave, and those after me will no doubt have forgotten where food came from, will not be able to tell you that walnuts grow on trees, or that pickles began as cucumbers on dirt-lashed garden vines.

The owner, a tall, broad-shouldered, middle-aged man, greets us in the foyer with menus. The lights are low and on each table a lighthouse lantern glows. The floor's been polished to such a shine that the lighthouses pool in the wood and beckon the drowning diners. My brothers tell the host how our mother had danced here three-quarters of a century ago. Joel requests the circular booth that fronts a waiter's station, so we can be near the dance floor, where a jazz band is warming up. A saxophonist solos. I smell black walnut trees in the notes; the nut peel's tartness spices the air.

"Now, looking at the menu specials," Joel starts out, when the waitress, a dark-haired, middle-aged woman, comes to the table with a basket of rolls and potato bread. "What would you suggest?"

She smiles widely. "Well, what are you in the mood for?"

I don't tell my brothers that I keep Luther's studio portrait near my desk next to a photograph of Florence. Nor do I mention Florence having told me that "Luther really loved me," and in the next sentence, "Phil was gone a lot." Luther had been the love of her life. My grandfather did not approve of him, and that made him dangerous. Czech like her, part of the Worley family, and in the photograph, he's handsome in his officer's Air Corps uniform. A pilot of the B-10s, those flying coffins, his blue eyes large, a light mustache on his upper lip, and a cigarette, maybe a Lucky Strike, between his index and middle finger, his thumb triggered at the filter as if to flick. Gold wings above his left pocket, over his heart. His cap tilted rakishly, he's smiling without parting his lips, smiling with his inner light. People don't yet grin idiotically, trying to make up for their weary faces. Next to his portrait is Florence's. Her hair's worn Betty Grable-style, puffed bangs rolled under and longish side curls, and her lipstick must be red, as it picks up the camera's shine. But it's her mouth my eyes are drawn to; lips slightly parted, a glint of teeth, like a slip peeking from under the dress hem. Luther and Florence.

My brothers both choose barbecued pork ribs, and when it comes, the platter is drenched in a smoky hickory sauce and the meat so tender it falls off the bones. Joel and Brett nudge the first forkfuls of soft, warm flesh into their mouths.

"Oh, that's delicious, Brother," Brett says, lifting another forkful.

Joel chuckles, "Iowa's finest, Brother."

They moan after every mouthful; it is clearly the best pork rib they've ever eaten.

The fish I've ordered is disappointing.

⁂

We drive the U-Haul back to the Super 80, where the three of us will prepare for Florence's memorial tomorrow. Brett will give the eulogy and I'll read a piece entitled "Mother of the Fields." It is the first time since childhood the three of us will share sleeping quarters; Joel and Brett together in one double bed and me in another.

After opening the windows and turning off the a/c, Joel stretches out on the bed with his laptop. Brett leaves to practice the eulogy in the lobby. The breeze that wafts across the parking lot brings only heat; no new-mown hay, just edge-of-town, strip-mall heat. My left arm, the paralyzed one, starts to burn. I take two Advil, but the still, humid air intensifies the pain, until it feels like my arm is on fire in a barbecue pit. I think of the pork ribs. I ask Joel if we can turn the a/c on low because I'm in pain. It's the first Joel has heard of the acute chronic pain I've been in for decades. It's something I prefer not to talk about. *Some mistakes last forever.* On goes the a/c–low.

Brett has retrieved a box holding 30 years' worth of the letters I'd written my mother. The woman who threw nothing away had saved them all. In this letter, I am a college undergraduate, asking for more money than the weekly check she sends. Now I am in graduate school, wondering if she could please send me a check for my thesis photocopying. And soon I'm a VISTA volunteer needing glasses, or so I say, and when I'm working in Houston, I have to find money for a damage deposit. There seems no end to my wheedling, my cock-and-bull stories, my money-grubbing. It ends only after I turn 34 and move to New York City. My throat fills with a thickness I can't swallow; I am ashamed. Brett asks if I want to keep the letters and I say no. He mentions the darkness contained inside those envelopes, and then carries them away to the hotel dumpster and heaves them in. I find a letter my friend Cynthia had written to me in those early months after the shooting. I'll keep this one. These were the days when stamps were 8 cents, when college students could rent a drafty farmhouse for $180 a month. "This quarter I can spend $5.50 a week. Sunday, no, I didn't go to church. Well, the midterms are here. After realizing how much money has been spent so far and how little learned, I ate some popcorn. I called Vinton tonight and your aunt said, 'Stephanie had her jaw wired today and the tubes from her nose and mouth removed. She hasn't spoken yet and her left arm is paralyzed.'" In those early days after the shooting, my mother left me to the care of my aunt and uncle; it was too painful for her to be around me.

I hear her voice telling me of the hurt that my rebellion had visited upon her. Sentences spoken over the decades, letters written. *Thanks to you, young lady, keeping me awake with your running away, then getting stuck and making me Western Union you money, this 60-year-old woman still teaches school. It almost serves you right when Duke Hospital calls after midnight Thanksgiving Day to tell me that kid has shot you. I see that kid coming into the bathroom where you still comb your hair.*

He's right there stupid stupid kid with the gun, the long barrel slung from his hip. I can almost inch almost slide my finger inside it to stop it, but how can I in this no light to see by? I see only handprints standing in air, blood and steam keeps them just over the sink as if the tub had tried to stumble up and it is the lathe wall all that plaster falls from.

I practice reading "Mother of the Fields" silently.

⁂

Rogers' Grove Cemetery. We know intimately the country cemetery on a rolling hillside surrounded by fields. Our father found Rogers' Grove beautiful and asked that he be buried here. For the invited guests, we've set up ten folding chairs near the bell. The farm where we grew up lies three-quarters of a mile from here. Once, a white-steepled church stood here, where Florence was baptized; where my father's second funeral was held after his body had traveled by train from Chicago; where the great bell had tolled for my grandfather, church organist for years; where pastors preached sermons in Czech, and no crosses adorned the walls. The first generation from Bohemia remembered priests bearing crosses when they came to ferret out Bibles hidden in manure.

Ten people, out of almost a century of life, to remember Florence.

I came here often as a child. Florence behind the wheel, the Rambler climbing the hill. It would be close to dusk, and the green of the leaves pebbled with gnats and bluebottles. The trees would talk and I had to listen, just as the trees are talking now. Dusk was the cooling-off time of day. I would walk through my own dead forebears: my grandfather; the baby, Marjorie, my infant aunt who died in 1918 after seven days of life; past my great-grandparents, Josephine and the gruff Josef Telecky. My great grandmother, said to be tiny, came from Bohemia alone on a sailing ship, a ladies' maid who hardly spoke English. Even with all the hair pulled back from her face as the women wore it then, she was beautiful, my mother had said. At my father's grave, we would pull the weeds and fill the Lipton's tomato juice can with flowers. I might wander past the Swabs' headstone, the mother and father surrounded by five smaller stones–boys' and girls' names, their death dates all the same month, the same year. Was it cholera, measles, whooping cough, or diphtheria, the strangling angel?

"Mrs. Swab felt so bad after all her children died within days of each other that she tore the hair from her head," Florence had told me.

I would stop at the wooden Civil War marker; at the limestone marker of the Moses boy, who had hung himself.

This is what remains of my childhood.

⁂

None of the guests have arrived yet when my brothers and I pull into the cemetery; only the gravedigger, with his tractor and scoop, has beaten us. A man lasts seven years in the earth, according to Hamlet's gravediggers. Our gravedigger digs a shoebox-sized hole on the wrong side of the headstone which Florence bought at the same time she buried our father. The hole has to be dug again. Even so, there's no symmetry here: the 36-year-old groom, the 98-year-old bride; one buried, one cremated.

As my brothers confer with the gravedigger, I sit by the honeylocust tree and see in my mind's eye my father waking in this cemetery a half-century after his death. It's a story I've started but haven't finished. Filling his lungs with so many smells; rich, manure-tilled earth. A multitude of scents, so many that he'd have to lie with his eyes shut and listen. No car horns, no traffic. Iowa. The sun soaking into his face would feel delicious. A windmill creaking. The pine trees rustling, joined now by an oak, throwing its leaves and rattling its branches. He wouldn't have his eyeglasses, and since he was terribly nearsighted like I am, the headstone next to him, *Philip O. Dickinson, 1920–1956*, would blur. He'd be blinking at the sun. This must be the resurrection of the body, he'd think; this might not yet be the life everlasting, as he's so thirsty. It feels like there's dirt lodged in his throat and a metallic taste in his mouth. A mistake. Perhaps he'd been in the earth by accident. But it wasn't possible. A tractor grunts in the field, and a beeping sound, the likes of which he's never heard before. The palms of his hands itch, as if the flow of blood has been cut off. Hunger inside him grows. Buzz of wasps. He tries sitting up. He's stiff. Rogers' Grove Cemetery. Florence's folks live a mile from here.

He's almost blinded. The green of the corn–he's never seen such green. As a conservation biologist, he knows how green is made. Chlorophyll. But it's unnatural, and everywhere he looks, there is corn. What happened to the ditches? Why, the corn seems ready to eat him, the corn looks like it wants to run after him. The corn seems to have teeth. He stands, looks at what he's wearing. His wedding ring is missing, as are his glasses, his billfold.

The Trees Are Talking

The guests are arriving. The first to park their car are Jim and Bess Telecky, my first cousin and his wife. Jim, a retired engineer, is twenty years older than my brothers and me. My brothers hug Jim, whose father was Florence's older brother. Jim, the same man they shrank from as boys, they greet with warmth. He is so stately and strong-jawed, and while we were still children, he was already a man and a father. In high school, Jim lived with my grandparents, and his Boy Scout uniforms haunted the farmhouse attic, along with his trumpet and his textbooks of bridge-building hieroglyphics. Back then he was called *Jimmy*. His voice sounded stern to our ears, calling his daughters to come or go, to eat or leave. We wondered if this was what a father was, someone whose words were to be obeyed. His two daughters became three, then four–Victoria, Rebecca, Deborah, and Teresa–names abbreviated in the American mid-20th Century style to *Vicky, Becky, Debby, Terry.*

I embrace Bess, and picture Thanksgivings at the farmhouse, Bess on the settee, pregnant, in her pink maternity smock, inky-black eyes and hair, not dark brown, but what Florence called *blue-black*. Full Czechs were either blue- or black-eyed, and their hair blond or black. Only half-Czechs like me sported *manure-brown* eyes and hair.

Bess's voice radiated kindness; her words would sometimes warble like a bird's chirp. Her sweetness had made me feel special. Now white-haired, her black eyes still shine in her smooth face. An Iowa face ages as if it is a pasture to lie down in, while East Coast faces (except for Jill Hoffman and those at the glass-table workshop) age as if caught on a high-speed treadmill. And Jim, at 80, is still a handsome, broad-shouldered man, but no longer unapproachable.

The second car to pull up belongs to Dr. Terry and Pamela Hopper, Aunt Pat's daughter and her husband, the oral surgeon. Terry holds the black iron gate open for Pamela, who is using a cane, having just had ankle surgery. "Oh, Stephy's here," Pamela says, upon spotting me between my brothers. I am wearing a blue, sleeveless A-line dress, a Kmart special, but a pretty one that Florence had approved of. "A beautiful dress," she'd said. "Hang it up. Don't just throw it like a rag over the chair. Let me iron it for you." A world away from the halter top and ripped jeans I had worn at 18, with the *bug of fear* drawn in magic marker on the knee.

Pamela has lost weight and looks shorter than I remember. I ask about her surgery. No one has yet mentioned Florence, whose ashes reside in a canister and a small crate stamped *School of Anatomy/University of Iowa.* Pamela, six years older than me, fills me in on the surgery performed by the best orthopedic surgeon in Iowa City, a good friend of Terry's. She is proud of her husband, an eminent professor at the University of Iowa's School of Dentistry.

Terry joins us under the hickories and puts his arm around Pamela. The sun splits the leaves and warms my face. They are children of the early '60s; the teased hair with poodle clips, pointy-toed flats, cigarette skirts, and form-fitting mohair sweaters. They had escaped the Jimi Hendrix siren call. To burn yourself out like a butane guitar solo. Pamela and Terry's youth still had structure. By the time I arrived in college, sororities were passé and for the straight kids; even participating in graduation ceremonies was considered unhip. For my degrees, the diplomas always arrived via the U.S. mail. The girls in my generation parted their hair in the middle like two curtains, put on jeans, and, for the next decade, never wore dresses.

Diane Buresh arrives alone. The daughter of my mother's first cousin and the granddaughter of Josie and Joseph, she's in her early 50s, a pharmacist, with the exotic, slanting blue eyes of the Buresh clan. A child of her mother's pre-menopause, an autumn crocus, ten years separated her from her brothers, the fraternal twins, Dale, a blue-eyed blond, and Dennis, black-eyed with black hair. Both were gentle, soft-voiced men who married once and well, who built subdivisions on Buresh land. Heavy smokers, both died in their early 60s, within a year of each other. Bess's sister is Dale's widow.

I kiss Diane and tell her how sorry I am about the twins. Bess has joined us. "It's terrible," Bess says, "to see my sister alone and without Dale. I remember the day they married."

I, too, remember their wedding at the country church. The bride and groom were our prince and princess; just graduated from high school, they shimmered in their beauty. I was a 9-year-old ugly duckling, wearing a second-hand recital dress, white anklets, and crooked bangs. Most wondrous of all was the three-tier wedding cake, decorated with lilies and lace, served in the church basement. I ate one piece of white cake, with its inch of frosting, and then a second. I gorged on handfuls of pastel mints and salted nuts, and washed the feast down with coffee. I filled my little girl's purse with mints. Czech church weddings offered no dinner or drinks, no DJs or bands.

Last come the Skalskys, the farmer millionaires, who live a quarter-mile up the road. Unapologetically fleshy her whole life long, and having survived valve-replacement surgery (one of the valves in her heart was born in the body of a sow), Betty's eager to live a full one hundred years. She looks the same as she did when she visited Florence for the last time. Betty arrives in a beat-up pickup driven by Steven, her cranky, snappish son, who, like his father, rails against the government, the neighbors, the roads, his son, and his grandson, who, when male visitors come, invites them into the barn to talk. *The barn, where all conversation between real men takes place, far from female ears.*

These are the remnants of my clan, those of my generation and of my mother's. The Telecky and Buresh sides of our heritage both represented. Except for her children, these are cousins and nieces and nephews, not the relationships of sinew and gut and menstrual blood. Mother, father, brothers, sister all have been gathered into the earth. She was the last of her family to die. Three of her siblings lived into their mid-90s and one brother died in his 80s, the one who died young. Good genes, Florence had always said.

Brett asks all those gathered to bow their heads and ask God's blessing. He leads us in the opening prayer. He speaks of Florence's unbreakable faith in a Divine Creator, a faith that had a penchant for sermons, choir singing, a quiet belief, a structured one. Not a clapping-and-speaking-in-tongues faith, not the boisterous kind, where the spirit starts moving and the fainters get to their feet and dance. Yet, he talks of her adventurous spirit; her taking the bus to California after her first year of college to be a nanny for a rich family, how the baby would not stop crying unless my mother pushed her in the stroller up and down the sidewalk, how the crying baby grew up and became a famous newspaper columnist.

His voice strong, it carries from the black iron fence, past the water pump, to the tumbled- down outhouse at the edge of the cemetery that, year after year, tumbles no farther. There, sagging between the hickories and basswood, the gray-shingled two-seater outhouse, roof vined with wild grape, stays. Perhaps the vines are holding it in place.

A year after Florence's death, the ashes, the grit, what she was made of, waits in its container to enter the earth. No one seems interested in the shoebox-sized hole and the urn. Her death occurred a year ago and Florence was old. With a body and a coffin, it is different, more potent. There's the pale, unmoving face; the hair said to grow into the coffin satin once the lid closes; the last look that draws the mourners.

Brett speaks of Florence's daring spirit lasting into her old age, how she wanted to learn and keep her mind alive. My mother had attended many an Elderhostel, those three-day not-for-credit classes for seniors given on a variety of topics, from cosmology to Willa Cather, on college campuses all over the Midwest. In one class, students were asked to write an essay about a memorable summer, one that truly stood out in their lives, and to use the strict essay form.

⁂

Florence's audaciousness. I am thinking of the essay she showed me, written when she was 76. Of all the summers of her life, the one she had spent in Summer Lake, Oregon, is the one she picked. Ninety miles from Bend, the nearest large town, she and my father live in a hunter's cabin with no running water or electricity (except for a generator that works two hours a day). Seven hunter's cabins between a dried-up lake and the low-lying Ponderosa Mountain Range, where Phil is interning on a pheasant-feeding project for the State of Oregon.

Florence prepares their meals on a wood-burning cookstove. Phil sometimes watches her hanging their washed clothes on an outside line between spruce trees. She irons his trousers with flat irons heated on the stove. Before dawn, he goes to the pheasants, and as the sun comes up, she steps outside behind the bleached gray cabin to ease her stomach and throw up. She is sure he loves the pheasants more than he loves her. What is it about those birds that draws him? There are no books here. She writes letters. No cars pass on the two-lane highway. Sometimes a truck. *We could use the electricity for lights only–that is, when the generator was working. I would try to break the monotony by taking ice-cream bars out to Phil that I purchased at the store, and thus spend some time with him while he worked.* She walks into the store, rubbing her hands over the wooden counter. Behind the cash register stands the owner, Myrtle, a lean woman, one side of her neck shorter than the other, who tilts her head to the left. Florence is surprised to see the tawny eyes in the woman's face, like a goat's golden orbs. The walls of knotty pine stare at the Oh Henry! peanut clusters and Burma-Shave. She asks for two vanilla bars coated in chocolate and watches the ice's breath rise from the freezer. The woman tells Florence that her husband drives a truck to Bend for supplies; sometimes he's gone for weeks. Myrtle runs a lunch counter, where she serves sandwiches. Some truckers like to eat their hamburgers raw. The woman asks Florence how she is. Myrtle, hewn out of this scrub and dust, is as stringy and plain as Florence, filling with child, is comely. Blooming.

She can hear the birds through the open window, where the dry air rattles the screen. Pheasants, wild fowls of the ground, how they flock together and delicately whisper. Is that why he loves them? Florence must hurry to the canal before her ice cream melts. The life inside her makes the sound of a pheasant. Will he mind if she carries him ice cream? Will he be angry if she interrupts the feeding of a pheasant? She feels a bubbliness, the fullness in her stomach a growingness.

Brett does not talk about the English teacher who had asked, "Do I spell *immediately* with one or two m's?" Joel does not attest to "Do you think we would have let her live in an apartment facing a parking lot for twenty years if she didn't make you feel so awful about yourself? She just starts in, beating up on herself and then beating up on you." I do not confess to haranguing her for money until she cried out, "I'm human. I'm human too." Or the many times she said, "You will dance on my grave." Yet, she would have cut her body into pieces to feed her children.

Florence and Phil together again; she is pregnant with my oldest brother. The hunter's cabins rise up with the sun. I can see my father carrying water to the pheasants. As he walks toward the dry canal, he stops and listens to their cooing and gossiping. The beautiful males and their dowdy ladies are already waiting. His Florence, still in her nightgown, a robe tied over it, walks to the outdoor hand pump for water. There is birdsong. The music of dryness rubbing itself against rock and scrub brush, the music of Ponderosa pines shifting in their blue-black feathering. Her eyes are blue; her hair, auburn; her body, European. I will let them live their day. Later I'll leave them here in the dark, where they lie together on the green-checked sleeping bag. They will dream. Nights, the mule deer, with their shy, mournful eyes, melt away. The pheasants too, their throats full of the shivering woods, vanish. The future has not happened.

Káva House

My brothers and I drive down Hwy. 965 to Swisher and park behind the Káva House & Café, where Brett has made reservations. Inside, the hardwood floors gleam and flowers spill out of Ball jars. I know Florence would approve of this family-run restaurant, with its buffet sideboards and tables set with thick farmer's silverware. She would especially approve of the menu's reasonable prices.

Swisher is one of the rare unspoiled small towns that used to dot Iowa and the Midwest. On the many bus trips I took from New York City to Cedar Rapids, I saw fewer quaint hamlets off the beaten track. No matter whether interstate or two-lane, strip shopping centers followed the highway–Jeep-4x4s, Kwik Fills, Smoker's Outlets, Boss Mini-Storages, and Go Go's Gas Pumps. Karaoke while you dine at Cozumel's Mexican Cantina. The Divine Infant of Prague Church wedged between Foxy's Den and Fluff n' Puff Laundry. Swisher used to thrive with independent banks, groceries, drugstores, and grain elevators. Actual commerce. Now you find an arts & crafts store, a health food store, and two cafés. The grain elevator endures.

We take our places at a long table in the enclosed porch. The remnants of our clan soon arrive to break bread and remember Florence. I sit between Diane Buresh and

Jim Telecky, the twinned Buresh/Telecky streams of my mother's ancestral blood. Across the table, Betty orders *The Virginia*, and her son, Steven, the *All Beef Made-Right*; Pamela, the *Hammie Sammie*: cured ham, pineapple, and spinach on whole-grain bread. Although I am in the land of the meat eaters, I select the *Cranberry-Walnut Salad*. Soon our orders arrive. The food is plentiful and delicious, yet the conversation feels muted, as we are strangers to each other. Betty, with her love of talk, fills the holes. Apparently, she finds the flutter of words exiting her mouth more soothing than the smoked ham and melted Swiss on her plate. She regales us with details of her grandson's and great-grandson's tractor-pull tournaments.

"Shay and Animal will be competing in the Iowa State Fair Tractor Pull," she says. Her complexion was, and remains, an Irish cream.

The men at the table banter about the rules of the tractor pull.

"So, is Shay's tractor modified with a drag-racing engine or jet turbine?" Joel asks, taking a sip of his iced tea. Rare is the topic that doesn't excite his curiosity.

"He's got a diesel engine in there," Steven tells us, his deadpan face breaking into a near-smile. "These sleds the tractors pull weigh tons. So you win by maybe a thousandth of an inch."

"How many times has Shay completed a full pull?" my brother says. "I mean, the course is only 30 feet long."

"Maybe so, but it's the hardest sport in terms of sheer strength. Shay has never made a full pull, but Animal's got the record."

I lean on my elbow over the walnuts and cranberries, picking them free of the greens. This is not the talk of mourning or remembrance. All these people at the table knew me before I was shot; they knew me as a child and then an adolescent with two working arms; they knew the *before* Stephanie and, so, around them, I am conscious of being the *after* Stephanie. We are waiting for the conversation to get interesting, something piquant. Did any of these people love Florence as my brothers and I did? Mother had been more reserved than her sister, Aunt Patsy, who had been a great favorite with us all.

The sky outside the enclosed porch darkens, as if the heaviness of depression, what Florence fought against all her life, is dragging the clouds down. Or a swarm of grasshoppers from the 1930s has returned to turn the day pitch-black. Lightning crashes; the lights flicker and then go out. Wind bends the trees, pulling the willows by their green hair, snapping branches from the hardwoods and sending them across the parking lot. Wind drives the rain into the Káva House's picture window with such force, it sounds like shotgun pellets. Is Florence's shade finally leaving this earthly realm? Perhaps her spirit has stayed close to her body, watching over it in the School of Anatomy, and only now is she moving on. Folklore and religion tell us that there are atmospheric disturbances when the spirit leaves for the next sphere.

I think of the storm the night my grandfather died.

He had been carrying a bundle of newspapers to burn outside in the chimney fireplace. My grandmother went to the sink to wash the dishes. She looked out the window and saw her husband of fifty-two years keel over into the grass. She rushed out, screaming "*John*." In that moment of falling, he'd crossed over into the black land. He'd left behind his flesh, and my tiny grandmother could not budge it. She called the Skalskys to come–Betty, the nurse, and Eugene, the strong arms. They carried my grandfather into the living room and laid him on the settee. The lane was soon filled with cars. Frederick, Vlasta, Florence; his children had come to be with their *folks*, a word for parents that has since rusted with disuse. My grandfather lying there, with his head of shining white hair, in his overalls and flannel shirt, hands resting on either side of his body. All the work those hands had done. I was 6 years old and unafraid of the motionless man on the settee. I listened to the orchard, to the insects with their tiny saws, and to the leaves bathing in the water trough. They had all belonged to my grandfather, and he to them–the apple branches– the pansies planted around the house in the shape of butterflies. It was late afternoon when the hearse drove into the lane; the undertaker had come for him. My grandfather left the farm with his dignity intact, himself until his last breath. We felt his absence the moment his body was taken. My grandmother could hardly speak. Not yet dusk when the sky went gray and thunder shattered the farm quiet. Then lightning struck my grandfather's favorite apple tree, and the leaves lit up blue-white before they turned to fire.

And now, sitting in the Káva House, I listen to the frightened trees bend, holding on as the thunder booms and the wind shakes them. I picture men in the scattering leaves, men of Florence's past; men she had danced with, those she had tended in the Red Cross. In the blown-away forest, her phantoms are clad in dungarees and army T-shirts; in the rushing away there are cloudless days. Just as suddenly as the wind came up, it dies away. The lights flicker back on, our forks move back to our plates, and the sweet potato French fries find their ketchup. All's right in the Káva House.

My older cousin, Jim, starts to speak. "Stephy, those two grandparents of ours were extra-special. I lived with them on the farm in high school and, later, when I started college. I used to go to the dances in Ely and, once, I got back to the farm late–around 3:00. I tiptoed in, hoping I wouldn't wake anyone, and I managed to get upstairs and into bed. The house stayed quiet, and I thought I'd made it. But in the morning, when I went down, your mother and grandmother were in the kitchen making breakfast and your mother started singing *I could have danced all night.* She knew, all right."

⁂

We drive through the countryside, the three of us together; it is likely the last time my brothers and I will be together in Iowa. I will be mourning Florence for the rest of my days. Who else drove the Rambler with the window rolled to guard against drafts; who else saved the Green Stamps that came with the gas fill-up, religiously pasting them into the books, hoping to have enough for a free toaster? Who rushed into our rooms in the middle of the night, shutting our windows when it began to rain? Always, she watched over us; she hung on to her life so she might still protect us, and now her body no longer stood between her children and death. Florence's *American Century* was over. Now we stand before death; soon our turn will come. Over to LaGrange Pharmacy; Me Too Market; the Paramount Theater, with its lush velvet drapes; Bezdek's Flower Shop; the cold-storage furrier, where the mannequin had worn the same mink stole for as long as I could remember. I will mourn Iowa; the lost family farm, the patchwork quilt of fields, the frogs and the bumblebees. It is left to me to remember until forgetfulness washes over the heartland.

"That was a great story Jim told," Brett says as we drive. *"I could have danced all night."*

A mother who missed nothing.

"Florence"
Oil on canvas by Jill Hoffman
18" by 36", 2013

Stephanie Dickinson, an Iowa native, lives in New York City. Her novels *Half Girl* and *Love Highway* and novella *Lust Series* are published by Spuyten Duyvil. Her other books are *Corn Goddess, Road of Five Churches, Port Authority Orchids, Heat: An Interview with Jean Seberg*, and *The Emily Fables*. Her work has appeared in *Best American Nonrequired Reading* and received multiple distinguished story citations in the *Pushcart Anthology, Best American Short Stories,* and *Best American Mysteries.*

Acknowledgments

Thank you to the following journals that originally published these stories, sometimes in slightly different form:

"Bluebeard of the Sticks" was introduced as "Hunger Wafers" in *Big Muddy*.

"Dementia Mother" was introduced as "May Snow" in the *Antigonish Review*.

"Townies" originally appeared in *Dogwood*.

Other Books from Rain Mountain Press

A Blanquito in El Barrio by Gil Fagiani (poems)

Adrift in the Vanishing City by Vincent Czyz (stories)

Asking My Liver for Forgiveness by Rob Cook (poems)

Blitzkrieg by John Gosslee (poems)

Carry On by Chris Belden (novel)

Church of the Adagio by Philip Dacey (poems)

Cities Hidden By Rain by Edgar Cage (poems)

Corn Goddess by Stephanie Dickinson (poems)

Diary of Tadpole the Dirtbag by Rob Cook (poems)

Dirty Sheets by The Poet Spiel (short stories)

Eilat by Luna Tarlo (novel)

Escape to Nowhere by Flower Conroy (poems)

Force of Flesh by Linda Tieber (poems)

Graduating from Eternity by John Goode (poems)

Insect Dreams by Rosalind Palermo Stevenson (novella)

Kafka at Rudolf Steiner's by Rosalind Palermo Stevenson (single story)

Kiss/Hierarchy by Alexandra van de Kamp (poems)

Lightning's Dance Floor by Ronald Wardall (poems)

Long Way Back to the End by Paul B. Roth (poems)

Mosquito Operas by Philip Dacey (poems)

Mostly Beethoven by Jiří Klobouk (single story)

My Father's Window by Mary Maya Hebert (non-fiction)

No Brainer Variations by Jim Cory (poems)

Road of Five Churches by Stephanie Dickinson (short stories)

Rooks by Gil Fagiani (poems)

So Late Into The Night by Elinor Nauen (long poem)

Songs for the Extinction of Winter by Rob Cook (poems)

The Absent by Rosalind Palermo Stevenson (novel)

The Complete Cinnamon Bay Sonnets by Andrew Kaufman (poems)

The King of White-Collar Boxing by David Lawrence (memoir)

The Lost River by David Chorlton (poems)

The New York Postcard Sonnets by Philip Dacey (poems)

The Short Imposition of Living by Matthew Keuter (poems)

The Taste of Fog by David Chorlton (novel)

Third Wife by Jiří Klobouk (short stories)

Under Taos Mountain by Penelope Scambly Schott (poems)